The hard hitting, realities in this book are very real. However, in an effort to protect the characteristics of certain individuals, there has been, some name and storyline modifications transcribed throughout this manuscript.

The authorized usage of poetry in this book were granted by Shawonna Wynn and are all copy written excerpts from the Greater Purpose Collection, distributed through Voice Of Silence Publishing, Inc.

Cover Design: Brandon Wiggins Photography

Cover Photo: Brandon Wiggins

My *Happiness* is My Sanity

Neffe and Shawonna Wynn

authorHOUSE®

My *Happiness* is My Sanity

Acknowledgments

I want to thank God for always covering me. After re-visiting the events of my life, God sent Angels to watch over me and protect me. To my children, always know that mommy loves you. You are my motivation. To my family; thanks for all your support and guidance. I ABSOLUTE-LY love you!

A special thanks to my editor Clark Triplett for all your hard work.
To my writer; Shawonna Wynn, who has become a friend and confi-dante.

The Posh Management Group; who encouraged me to tell my story and hung in there with me through the process. Willie Triplett you are some-thing else. My Love, Soullow for supporting me through the long days and hours. A special thanks to all my relatives, friends and fans for all your support.

AuthorHouse™
1663 Liberty Drive, Suite 200
Bloomington, IN 47403
www.authorhouse.com
Phone: 1-800-839-8640

First published by AuthorHouse 2/6/2009

ISBN: 978-1-4389-3981-0 (sc)
ISBN: 978-1-4389-3982-7 (hc)

Printed in the United States of America
Bloomington, Indiana

This book is printed on acid-free paper.

Contents

Hell-A-Mad

Are you serious?
What the fuck do you mean I'm ghetto?
Why? Because I get loud when I feel as though I'm backed into a corner, or is it the fact that I'm not afraid to express my emotions?

Fuck that! Who the fuck are you to judge me?
You can't tell me about me.
Nobody can tell me about me.

You know what, at this point, it doesn't matter what you think about me.

And you know why? You know why?
I'll tell you why!
I'm hurt!
I'm hurt because my momma wasn't there the way I thought she should be.
Because I was raped at 9, and while my cousins were forced to watch, there was no one around who could protect me.
Because as a teen, I was misled by a married man, twice my age

And I'm angry!

I'm angry because my husband left me for my first (fucking) cousin. Tell me, how the fuck does that work?

And the cold part about it is, before that bastard even had a chance to leave me I left myself. I was the one that allowed us to engage in multiple partner activities on account that I wanted our marriage to work.

How the fuck does that work?

I'm saying, how do you do that? How do you do that?
How do you love a man so much that you turn your back on yourself?

1

I'm tired, and this bull... you know what!
My Heavenly Father has a plan for me though, and I may not be able to see it right now but in His time, it's going to all come together.

So yea, I fuck up sometimes but I never said I was a saint, and God never said I had to be perfect. I will say that I'm in the fire right now and everything is going to get better, and even though I drink a lot right now I am not going to be known as the alcoholic mascot forever.

Let me ask you a question.
How do you cope?

Being the oldest of 7, and not having a chance to truly grow up with any of your brother's or sister's? How do you come to grips with wanting a mother's love so bad, that you run away from the home that your grandmother is raising you in, to live on the streets doing whatever it takes to survive besides prostitute, while watching the woman that birthed you sell her ass and get high?

How do you get past the pain of being betrayed and learn to forgive? And most importantly how do you forgive yourself?

When do you stop breaking down so that you can stand up for yourself?

What I need you to understand is, you can't spray paint dirt and call it candy coated, it is what it is. I'm just telling it for what it is. That's why I'm writing this book because too many people are out to lunch on this fake shit, man.

I'm going to give it to you raw and uncut and if you don't appreciate it, you can kiss my ass.

I know every body has a story, so I don't need a pity case. I'm just saying this is some real shit. It's like the best untold story too familiar to be untold, too relatable to be overlooked, and too close to be ignored any longer.

It's not a story, it's life

Either you're wit it or you're not....

CHAPTER 1

A HAUNTING REVELATION

REALITY CHECK

Welcome to the real world
Where the bills are overdue
And the funds are low
Where STD'S are not the only high risk
Of the parental guidance underflow
Where it's hard to catch a full course meal
But the contraband exchange
Is like a shopping cart with flat wheels
Blocked off by the wants of perfection
Waiting for your sacrifice
Fresh handed or collection
Where it's a struggle to do right
And a skill to live unrighteous
Judge not the form of temptation
But the freedom of truth is priceless
Behind locked minds dreams are scandal by worries
And hopes are a hostage of stress
Everyday is a short come, come up
Scheduled for the hidden wish express
Where failure is (no) mystery
And all surrounding situations are a mess
Where clouds cover history
Staging curiosity to embrace bound and oppressed…S.W.

Being raised in a household that didn't believe in most traditional holidays, I missed out on a lot of bonding memories that many carry along their journey of life, through a cherished treasure of love. It didn't necessarily sit well with me, but like everything else that life forced upon my childhood, I took it for what it was. Ironically, the one holiday I was allowed to enjoy turned out to be as traumatizing as the demon influenced masquerades that paraded the streets with unforeseen tricks and/or treats.

I don't remember the exact year, but it was a Halloween that I would never forget. I had to be around 8 or 9 years old, and as I think back, it actually all began with an episode that adjusted my reality two days beforehand. Leading me into a spirit of somber brokenness, through a domino effect of resentment and anger, it turned out to be a life altering incident that severed my every circulating motive to care. In fact, my stomach still turns as I recapture visuals of the fright night, when my mother showed up at my grandmothers house tattered, worn out, and desperate for food.

My grandmother wasn't home, and my grandfather refused to give my mother a break of any sort. I remember the two of them arguing back and forth, as my grandfather insisted that my mother went away, and my mother stated soundly the rights to be in her mothers' house. Tensions raised as they continued to fuss and cuss with my mother making her way to the kitchen, and as she leaned over to look for something to eat, my grandfather slammed the refrigerator door right on her head.

Taking on my mothers' agony as if my own, I could feel my soul shatter while everything inside of me collapsed with screams of pleading despair. I was a young girl, but I knew right from wrong, and as I wailed from witnessing my mother endure the excruciating pain, I didn't understand how anyone could be so cold and heartless. Mentally, a fuse erupted that triggered sensations of rage, and the more blood I saw pour out of my mothers' ear, the more I disbursed into an emotional wreck.

Unable to gather myself, I cried endlessly because even though my grandmother was taking care of me, my mother meant the world to me, and watching her being mistreated like that, just didn't make sense. My grandfather ran her off like a stray dog, when all she wanted was something to eat. At the time, I could not comprehend any reasoning behind his actions, and the whole situation left me very discontent. That incident manifested an evolving reality that magnified my perspective views of darkness through a whole new light.

Carrying over into Halloween, I don't think anyone noticed the shield of frustration that weighed heavy upon my chest. For most, I guess everything went back to normal, but speaking on behalf of myself, time dragged me through every minute. I could not shake the traumatizing playback out of my mind, as my mothers affliction continued to hunt me like a reoccurring nightmare. No matter how I tried to block out the presentation, it was a repetitive feature that strengthened the effects of horror, by weakening me into a secluded shell.

Physically, I was around, but there was no other part of me that could be accounted for, as I wondered through my grandmothers' house in a trance. It was as if I had been seized by the devastation, and my character transitioned from a child trying to prove her worthiness for love, to an embodiment of sullen mystification. I withdrew from being the little girl who extended her best to please everyone, and began to embrace a newly birthed evil that represented everything despite, my normal behavior. I was more than eager to compliment the festivities of hell night, with my awakened wickedness.

We didn't have much money to put towards purchasing masks, or anything else for that matter, so with a brewing imagination, and a few items from my grandmother's wardrobe, I dressed up like a witch. Finally I was ready to fly free, and as the hour approached for me to scout the neighborhood for countless opportunities on a candy hustle, I looked forward to what the night had in store. Not only because it was a rare chance to interact with the outside world, but within me was a craving for drama, driven by a vengeance that had begun to eat away my morals, and it had yet to be satisfied.

In between the innocence of my nature, greeting lit porches for handouts, the monster breeding inside of me plotted to make sure that someone else would reap the effects of my misery. My, "just cause" motivation was a previous Halloween that replayed me as a victim to an ambush, and while I vividly relived the experience of being knocked to the concrete as my pillow case of goodies was snatched away, I knew exactly how to pacify my devilish appetite. I know it sounds bad, but it felt good, as I flip flopped from vulnerable to villain with an absent conscious on a mission to menace the night.

Once the mischief had reared itself to an end, I went back to my grandmothers and as I entered along side a playmate cousin, it was like walking into a dungeon of gloom. Luckily, my cousin and I rounded up enough children's gold to keep us occupied, and as we bartered mounds of categorized sweets, laughter highlighted adventures of our evening. Of course it didn't take long for my mind to get restless, and with a bright idea, I decided that as a source of entertainment we could play with our Halloween bags over the stove.

It wasn't that I was fascinated with fire, I just wanted to show my cousin how the plastic would inflate, after capturing steam from the boiling water. Thinking it to be harmless, in no way did I intend for the demonstration to turn hazardous. Unfortunately, my thoughts did not dictate the outcome. However, thanks to my misfortunate multi-tasking ability, a slight motion with one hand, to reach a bag in another, managed to leave me scared for life. It all happened very fast, but somehow a loose bag caught hold of the pot, and as I tried to pull it away, the pot fell off the stove causing the hot water to gush across my stomach.

Ahhh…Sugar Honey Ice Tea!, The same house, same kitchen, and the same screams of pleading despair duplicated from a recent episode of torment. Only this time I didn't have to take on the agony because the uncontrollable cries from this excruciating pain, was absolutely for my own relief. My skin felt like it began to melt instantly, and I jumped and screamed until my grandmother ran in to see what happened, but when she realized what I had done, she belted a few hollers and screams of her own.

In a tone that offered no remorse, all I heard was, "Neffeteria Roshea Pugh", and all I could think was, "O Lord". My grandmothers' voice overpowered my trauma, and shifted me into a new direction of focus, because hearing her call out my full name meant that I was in some serious trouble. I knew that she was furious, and it didn't matter to her that I was a scorch away from a skin graph, so in addition to the 3rd degree burns, I was surely about to encounter another form of hurt.

Feeling the burn of both the boiling water, and my grandmothers boiling anger, proved that my idea to play with fire was definitely not one of my brightest. Surely, this was not quite the outcome that I had in mind. To top that off, besides beating the crap out of me, my grandmother wanted to teach me a lesson, and refused to take me to the hospital. In her sick and twisted effort to punish me, she not only allowed me to suffer, but she left me to deal with the pain and heal on my own.

Further more confirming her to be the witch I portrayed in costume, my grandmother showed no compassion. She went to the extreme, just to make it plain and clear that she could care less about my wounds, by ignoring me. In fact, the closest I got to receiving medical treatment was a glob of Vaseline. No E.R, no Doctor, no burn ointment, no bandage, no duck tape, just a thick coating of petroleum jelly and an insensitive, "That's what the fuck you get". You would think that I would have learned my lesson, but unfortunately as it will be relayed, I became a stickler for heat in many forms to come.

The healing process took a few months, and as I continued to peel away my scorched flesh, I uncovered wounds far beyond the surface in which the scabs appeared. Deep beneath the visual layers of what any tissue could scar, resided years of emotional injuries that had been unable to heal, because I spent my life blocking them out. It took me some time, but later in life, I realized that I had been fighting each and every day to find a sense of self worth, and security through all the inherited negativity that my bloodline proclaimed.

Assuredly more obvious than stated, that moment in time snapped me out of a sedated numbness, and brought forth a drastic discovery. Revealing that it wasn't just my grandmother neglecting to attend to my wounded needs, it wasn't just the beating that followed my self inflicted pain, and it wasn't just the echoes of my mothers cry for mercy, as her supposed loved ones unapologetically degraded her to be lower than the streets they forced her into. It was however just that and so much more, that subjected me to come face to face with the pain I had buried within.

Subsequently there was no more room to contain the turmoil that my life increasingly delivered, so I found it to be in my best interest to push all the pain outward. I decided that I didn't want to take everything that was handed for what is was anymore, and being that I had lost all respect for my grandmothers' household, I didn't. This was a decision that not only transformed me into a disruptive wild fire that spread uncontrollably, but with an, "I don't give a fuck" mentality, it was also the beginning of a life style that spiraled me into a classic case of self-destruction.

You see well before, I was transparently broadcasted across the airwaves, and into the hearts, minds, and spirits of many who have come to know me as "NEFFE", I was a little girl who spent her life searching for a place of peace, joy, and happiness. A place where I could genuinely love and be loved. A place where I knew I was cared for, and actually belonged. A place where I wouldn't have to always keep my guards up, because I would always be protected. Day by day I imagined myself disappearing from all of the circumstantial chaos bestowed upon my childhood, and I held on to my sanity by finding a place where I could hope.

It is important to me for you to understand that in the beginning stages of my life, I wasn't the loud and out of control individual that tantrums into an irrational rage just to get a point across. Nor was I always known for having the tendencies to spur off into a "drunken spectacle". Then again I had yet to be disappointed by my loved ones, raped of my innocence, betrayed by my lovers, or crushed by other tragic mishaps that tend to illustrate ones character, through a projection of distorted fragments.

I had yet to experience the amazing journey that would map out a path that bridged my fate into an accident waiting to happen. I had yet to run into the entrapments of dead ends, and I had yet to route through the detours, the potholes, or worn out pavement that contributed to the weariness of my stability. I wasn't prepared for the crash course that my quest would drag me through, but it was apart of my legacy nonetheless, and it is apart of my destiny to see it through.

Going back to as far as my memory replays itself my life has been, overwhelmed by complications. Yes, I've had some pleasant moments, but after about the third grade, I have been strung along from one episode of drama to the next, and through it all, I've come to the understanding that all is for a purpose. I have come to realize that I am just a messenger with a mainstream storyline that's tired of being overlooked, so as these pages reveal the hidden secrets of a tainted past, I encourage you to dig between the lines.

I dare you to open your eyes and see the unspoken pains and frustrations that plague many households within any given community, and discover the harmful creation of some hurtful situations. I challenge you to confront the disabling decisions that cause life long deficiencies for not just the decision maker, but more so the loved ones that bear the burdens of selfish choices. I forewarn that you, do not confuse reality with amusement as I expose a life un-edited, un-cut and un-fudged because before it became what it is today, this is my life, **THE WAY IT *WAS***

CHAPTER 2

STOLEN INNOCENCE

CONFESSION

My lust wasn't lusting for me
Wasn't paying me any attention at all
My yearn wasn't yearning for me
 I was learning to live
With no respect at all
My days wasn't shining for me
Shower's stormed
And rain never failed to fall
My life wasn't all about living for me
I was living to settle content to crawl
I was too close to the dirt
To see I could never stand
Because I never stood up too tall
What I sought showed no good for me
Winning in the lost soul of my life
I was boxed to fight endlessly
I thought I wanted more for me
I gained nothing to claim anything at all
I was downhill like a wind chill
On a dry day with no breeze
My existence had dropped
As my contamination rose to record breaking degree's
Damage was done and I was to…S.W.

Living with my grandmother was like a joke with no punch line, and the older I got I still didn't get it. During my infant year's I'm sure it didn't make much of a difference, but as I grew older something began to click, and I would often find myself saddened without explanation. It wasn't until I entered elementary school that I took notice to the other children who had something more than I could ever imagine, and I couldn't help but wonder that maybe a "mommy" was the answer to what my life had been missing because I only had Nanna.

Even though my grandmother had been keeping me from the time I was a baby, and her house supplied the only loving family that I had grown to know, I never really seemed to fit in. I didn't understand it right away, but as my comprehension increased, I began to ask questions concerning the blanks in my puzzled mind. I guess no one thought it to be worthwhile to tell me about the woman I would later learn to know as my mother, so whenever I asked I would be shunned away with a simple story of how she was sick and couldn't take care of me.

Of course, that didn't make things any better because if she was sick and couldn't take care of me, I needed to be taking care of her. My concern made me want my mother even more, and being that I insisted on finding out where she was, my grandparents finally broke down to tell me the truth. I never paid much attention before, but as they went into the description of this frail image, I was able to picture her in my mind, and I recalled the previous occasions in which I had seen her drop in.

I became overtaken by the hurt of realizing that the mystery woman who would show up from time to time, and disappear as fast as the winds that blew her in, was the void in my hollow heart. Indeed, I too had a "mommy", just like the other children, but unlike the other children, my mommy wasn't able to take care of me. My mommy had an infection and the illness that had kept her from being with me was nothing that I could help cure, because she was contaminated by life on the streets.

In the mean time, the children at school didn't hold back from making fun of me because they knew that I was living with my grandparents, and wanted to rub it in my face. I don't think it would have been so bad if my grandmother would not have gone out of her way to turn me into a total tease target. Being called "Nefferteria the Cafeteria" chuckled up enough annoyance, but once my grandmother decided to transgender my appearance by cutting my hair down to brush waves, the jokes free styled into a whole new level.

My self esteem was delivered straight to hell, all because my hair was too long and thick for my grandmother to deal with, and she acted as though combing it was going to send her to the grave. When my hair finally did grow back, she still refused to keep it up on a regular, and I began to feel like it was apart of her responsibility to make sure that I was insecure. Every so often she would take the time to braid and bead my hair, but other than that, as if it wasn't enough to nearly shave me into a skinhead, she would experiment with pineapple waves that made it look like I was sporting more of a science project than a hairstyle.

During this time, I began to feel as bad as the direction my life seemed to be headed. I could barely focus on class work with all of the degrading comments that the children were darting at me. In fact, I spent so much time trying to defend myself that it became almost impossible for me to uphold the good grades, my grandparents stressed. Perhaps, if I would not have been, stressed out by my grandmothers degrading makeovers, I would have been able to get along a little better. Then again, I don't even know if she realized that she instigated my frustrations, by providing the chisel in which was used unsparingly to chip away my, shy girl conduct.

The children continued to pick, and my confidence continued to fade with every malice remark that penetrated into my already shambled frame of mind. For a while, I tried to ignore the cruelties, and pretended that the words did not bother me, but the reality was that everything I heard cut me very deep. I held back from getting too out of hand right away because I knew my grandmother wouldn't hold back from getting into my ass, though eventually I made it my business to throw off a few stabbing jabs of my own.

As the years went by, my rampage at school collided with the frustrations within my family, and it began to seem as though I was caught in a cyclone. Each moment brought forth a conflict that forced a constant battle every which way I turned. I was fighting for piece of mind at my grandmothers' house, fighting for respect at school, and fighting for my life in between. Nothing was going right for me, and the more I attempted to be the co-operative nice girl, everything went wrong. Before I knew it, my grandmother was packing me up, and sending me to San Maria, California to live with my Uncle for a while. She thought that placing me into a different environment would calm me down.

I was feeling more and more out of place at my grandmothers' house, so for me this was a vacation long over due. By the time I arrived at my Uncle's, I needed as much of a break from my grandmother as she needed from me, and knowing that I had a break from those mean ass kids, helped me to appreciate the days to come. The change of scenery was exciting, and amongst other details that separated the two households, it was a sigh of relief to find out that the rules in which I had to abide were definitely not the same.

To say that my grandmother was strict would be an understatement, and the older I got the more she tried to keep me in the house, because she knew that in Brookfield anything was liable to happen. I was barely allowed to sit on the front porch, and asking to take a stroll through the neighborhood was like asking to take a trip overseas, so I was forced to expand my horizons through Television. My Uncle, on the other hand, had given me a freedom that stretched a little further than TV Land, and for the first time, I didn't have to be paranoid about walking down the block because of my grandmothers over protective nature.

I still didn't consider it as my home, but my Uncle's house was pretty cool. I especially enjoyed the fact that I was around cousins that were my age, and apart of the same dysfunctional heritage. This meant that I was able to blend in without feeling like a total outcast. I no longer felt isolated and alone, and the adjustment process smoothed over much easier than I ever expected. Then again, I didn't know what to expect because for so long I had been feeling like there was no one that I could relate to. I had no idea what it was like to have someone who cared enough to take the time to understand me, or even gave a damn about what type of turmoil I was dealing with on the inside.

Life began to look up for me, and being in a different atmosphere was more than a breath of fresh air, it was about time. Before I knew it, my happiness began to come naturally, and I didn't have to wish myself into a far away world of pretend just to have laughter, and joy without regret. I didn't have to disappear to a place where I could be accepted for who I was, without the frustrations of who I wasn't in the eyes of every one else, because I was appreciated for being me. I didn't have to escape the painful reenactments, and I didn't have to hide the sorrows of being taunted by hell raiser classmates. Not because they were miraculously erased from my memory, but for a brief moment I was able to experience living without dwelling on the disturbing incidents that stripped away my piece of mind.

Each day seemed to get better and better, and the weekends were even greater because my Uncle believed in working hard to play harder, so on Friday night's, he usually wouldn't make it back in until Saturday morning. That allowed my cousins, and I to stay up until we passed out. We would lay pillows from the couch across the living room floor, and wrap up in our own blankets while watching movies, and talking about a little bit of everything, and a whole lot of nothing that meant something to us. It was like our sacred campground, and as we shared amongst ourselves the pains that each of us buried alive, I slowly let my guard down.

Knowing the consequences of being the first to go to sleep, the four of us fought hard to out last one another. It was an unwritten rule of survival because between having mustard and ketchup put on your lips, and having your ears and nose tickled with spit twirled tissue, you were sure to be the last laugh. Especially, once the mayo that was generously plopped into your hand, landed on your face from a sudden reaction that urged you to impulsively wipe for a convenient knee slapping sight. I fell victim a couple of times, but being the prank didn't give as much satisfaction as being the prankster, so I would try my hardest to be "the last man standing".

I remember one evening in particular that stands out in my mind, and I didn't understand why it was happening, but I was being revisited by tormenting flashbacks that altered my mood into an emotional gloom. I held back from telling anyone because I didn't want to bother them with my silent torture, so while hoping that it would just go away, I tried to overshadow my anxiety with a mask of blended excitement. Considering that we all had an issue or two, my cousins didn't recognize that I was crying for help from the depths of my soul, and I didn't make it a point to bring it to their attention.

The night went on with my cousins and I attending to the usual commitment of channel flipping, and horse playing until each of us fell asleep, one by one. Even though I didn't remember falling to sleep, I knew I wasn't the first one down, so when I felt a hand reaching over my face, I didn't quite know what was going on. When I opened my eyes to catch the practical joker by surprise, I immediately went into a paralytic shock because I realized that it was not one of my cousins trying to decorate my face with condiments. It was a man who had no reasonable explanation to be inside of my Uncle's house.

I was totally caught off guard, and I couldn't scream because as soon as I parted my lips, black leather gloves muzzled over my mouth, and gripped my jaws. My eyes began to circle around to catch a focus of what was really going on, and I was unable to catch a breath to save my life. Once my blurry vision cleared, I noticed the paining eyes of my other female cousin, who was also pinned on the ground to the far right of me. As soon as I caught a glimpse of her face, I nervously looked over to the left of me, and made eye contact with my two male cousins, as they stood frozen by the fear of a pistol aiming for a point blank range, shot to their heads. Helpless in our actions, I didn't know what to think because this was no joke, and it definitely wasn't funny.

I laid there unable to move, and too restrained to defend myself while my cousins, were forced to watch as my sense of self was being raped away, by the fierce intents of a thief in the night. My body stiffened up like a corpse, and hot tears streamed like a leaky faucet down the sides of my head while my throat, became swollen from the trapped cries that were never to be heard outside of my own sound. My mind went into a shouting rage that pleaded, "HELP!, PLEASE STOP!, LEAVE ME ALONE!, and GET OFF OF ME!", but it didn't do any good because no one was there to help, and my attackers refused to listen. Repeatedly, I was tore into with violent strokes of guiltless aggression, and the only thing I could do was hope that it would be over soon.

I don't know how long the rape went on, but it seemed to have lasted an eternity. At some point, I do believe that I literally blacked out, because I don't even remember my violator getting off of me. All I can tell you is that, everything became a haze, and every face was just an image as I curled into a fetal position, and cried more tears from my well of agony. I don't know how long I laid there, and I can't tell you who was the first to show up on the scene. All I remember is being on that floor, wishing for the one person who wasn't anywhere to be found, and that was my mother.

Shelling into another sedated numbness, I went through the next couple of days in a state of shock. I felt sick, and I didn't want to be bothered with anyone. So, whenever I was asked about what happened, I would answer with vague and minor detail. My cousins were much more useful when it came to detailing the situation, and after giving the descriptions of the men who committed the crime, it turned out that they lived in the neighborhood. They actually knew my Uncle, they were aware of his routine, and they were familiar with the broken window that allowed them to enter the house with no problem.

The situation devastated my uncle, and even though action had been taken to prosecute the men, the feeling of guilt began to wear away his conscious. That's when my family came to the conclusion that it would be best for me to go back to my grandmothers' house. As I headed back to my grandmothers', I felt like I was born to be miserable, and once again I faced feelings that isolated me to be alone. In my mind, there was no one who could understand me, and even though my grandmother expressed her regrets, her sympathy was more like blame.

In my heart, I knew she loved me, but I don't believe she knew how to show it, because not once did she extend a hug to comfort me. Nor did she attempt to soothe away the pain by telling me that everything would be okay. For whatever reason she just was not an affectionate woman, and I learned to be okay with that. However, I still could not make sense of why I had to be unfairly punished for a crime that violated my innocence. Well, at least I was able to understand her reason for having burglar bars over every opening of the house.

Again, I was frustrated and angry and my life seemed to be flushing away right before my eyes. I didn't know what to do, so instead of accepting the devastations that abruptly impeded my life, I tried to make myself believe that everything was just a bad dream. I pretended as if the rape was not real, and my grandmother was not holding me hostage for being the victim of a heartless act. I didn't talk about it, I didn't deal, I didn't get over it, and I didn't heal. I just pressed it into the depths of my soul, and simply locked it away. At the same time, I also didn't realize that this was just a temporary fix to a long term problem, because I didn't remember that there was only so much that I would be able to take in before I went off.

My resolution for not allowing myself to be effected by the situation was obviously ineffective, and my temperament increasingly blasted off in short fused spurts. I did my best go through the days acting as though nothing was wrong with me, but the reality was that I was feeling like a worthless rag doll. I was suffering in plain sight, and no one was aware of the pain that was eating me up from the inside, while everyone around me questioned the disorderly conduct that I had seemingly acquired out of thin air. I was a child losing a battle to survive in a dead life, and I felt like nobody could look beyond my troubled acts to see.

In the mean time one of my Aunts, ended up with a place around the corner from my grandmothers' house, and she stepped in like a guardian to my rescue. Showing up not a moment too soon, she positioned herself as a mother figure in my life. Catering to the voids, and meeting the needs that I had been longing to be fulfilled. She was also able to provide much of what I felt like I had been missing in a mom. Don't get me wrong, her being there for me didn't replace the yearning that I had to be with my own mother, but for once in my life I was able to experience what having a mother was actually like.

She took time to talk to me, and express how much she loved me without blaming me for the corruption that my life encountered. She also tried to help me understand the illness that had been keeping my mother away from me, by letting me know that she too was battling the sickness in her own way. The more she began to spend time with me the more I was able to add pieces to the puzzle that I had been trying to figure out, for a very long time.

I began to attach myself to my Aunt because she played a major role in helping me to feel better about myself. Even though my bile attitude didn't seem to be getting any better, (right away). The more time I spent with her, I realized that there was something special about her, because she made me feel like I was equally loved, and cared for. That meant a whole lot to me because unlike my cousin who grew up with me in my grandmothers' house, she wasn't really my mother. Although fortunately for me, while she was around, she never neglected to treat me as if I were one of her own. She just did whatever she could to fill in the gaps, and made sure that I was not left out.

Eventually, I ended up staying with my Auntie, which worked out very well for me because I was able to be closer to my cousin Lesby. Lesby, was my Auntie B-B's daughter, but unlike her brother who grew up with me in my grandmothers' house, our relationship was developed on a totally, different level. She was more than just a female cousin, she was my favorite female cousin, and every time she would come to spend the night over my grandmothers, I was sure to have a good time.

In fact, being that my grandmother didn't have a big house, the 3 bedrooms that were available had to be shared between the 5 of us who lived there. This meant that my grandparents had one bedroom, my two boy cousins shared another, and I was left to sleep with whoever popped in at the time. Over the year's, I learned to make the most out of the arrangements. Especially when it gave me a chance to sleep with Lesby, because she opened me up to experience a side of me that I didn't even know existed.

I looked forward to the ways that she aroused me, and whenever I found out that she would be spending the night, a thrill of excitement shot through me like a super surged rush of "can't wait". Even though my Auntie was there to talk to me and give me comfort, Lesby knew how to calm me down by tapping into needs that I had no idea was there. It was an oddly pleasurable experience, but she would always supply the affectionate touch of female that I desperately craved, and now that I was living with her, I was satisfied to know that I would never have to miss out on the sensations of her secret touch again.

During the time that I lived with my Auntie things were okay, but I was so damaged that even with trying to be good, I continued to stir up complications. Some days I would be on my best behavior and on others, I would act out of the anger that permanently resided inside of me, and show out as bad as I felt. It wasn't long before I became too much to handle, and between my Auntie and my grandmother, they decided that it was time to call on additional help.

Before I knew it, a decision was made for me to be sent to live with a man that I had heard of, but vaguely knew. Initially, I wasn't very comfortable with the idea, but no one ever asked how I felt about the situation, and because he was my father I was expected to automatically go along with the program. From what I understood, I was his only child at the time and with overjoyed excitement, he accepted me into his home with no questions asked. I didn't get it right away, but for the sake of everyone involved he took a stand to uphold his responsibility as the father he never extended himself to be. So taking me in was his way of proving that he had finally grown up.

Living with my father allowed me to build a bond with him that I would have never imagined, in fact having a father was never, really that important to me. Of course, that was until I had a chance to be with my own. I can honestly say that our laughing and hanging together was time well spent, but I silently wondered how long it would be, before the drama kicked in. It wasn't that I had any doubts that he loved me, I just knew in my heart that the real test was being able to deal with the challenges that came along with me.

Totally clueless to the hardships and frustrations that he invited upon my arrival, my father considered me to be his pride and joy. His decision to pick up the slack of what he had walked away from nearly a decade prior, helped him to realize how much he had been missing out on, and all of a sudden his world revolved around me. He made sure that I was comfortable and did everything he could to accommodate me. Even to the extent of making sure that I had my own bed in my own room. He catered to me like, I was the center of his attention, and embracing the advantages that came along with being "daddy's little girl", I felt like the princess that he put me on a pedestal to be.

Two or three weeks passed by and my father went over his rules. However, just like every other rule that I disobeyed everywhere else, I broke them. I also broke the bed that he firmly instructed me not to jump on, but I jumped on it anyway. When the mattress fell through the bed rails sending me tumbling onto the floor, I was scared out of my mind. I didn't know what to do, so I created this bogus story about how I was going to the bathroom, and the bed just fell. I figured that since I was his darling little angel, and we were on such good terms, that there was no reason to press the issue.

Laying down the law, my father made sure to go over his rules once more, just to make sure that I understood that he meant what he said. The law was his thick reversible leather belt, and being that he had caught in a lie, each side took turns making its mark across my ass. The cold part about it is that before he actually whopped me, he gave me a chance to tell the truth, but because I was too afraid to let him know what really happened, I decided to stick to my story.

I didn't think to know that my father was already aware of what had taken place, and because he really didn't want to discipline me, he gave me an opportunity to be honest. Of course, that was just too much to ask of me. That day I found out that lying was one of the things he refused to tolerate, and I put him in a position to whop me for the very first time. I would say that it hurt him more than it hurt me, but that man had a strong, arm swing. At that moment, every landing lash exchanged my warm welcome with a stinging regret.

After the bed incident I still managed to get into trouble, but there is only one other time that I can recall my father actually whopping on me. This time the rule that I broke was having company in my bedroom when I had been, repeatedly instructed not to do so. I don't think that it would have been such a big deal if I would have had a little girl in my room, but being that it was a little boy, my fathers girlfriend, made the situation out to be a huge ordeal. She started fussing about what she thought, and how my father should handle me in the situation. I on the other hand, didn't care for this particular girlfriend in the first place, so since she wouldn't stop rambling on about what was going through her mind, I cocked back and punched her in the face.

I can't tell you what I was thinking, but I swung and connected, and it felt good. Of course, she ended up giving my ass a proper beat down. As soon as it was all said and done, my father was once again put in a position to tag a little tail of his own. As time would tell this was the last time my father disciplined me. I will also say that it was the "final straw" or "the straw that broke the camels back", because not only did he beat me, he got rid of me. He packed me up and shipped me to a group home in Richmond, California.

My grandmother wouldn't take me back, my Auntie was dealing with issues within her own family, and my Father would have had better luck riding a wild bull then keeping up with me. So away to the professionals I went. I couldn't pretend enough to ignore the fact that I was being tossed around like a hot potato, and it hurt. I felt like everyone was giving up on me, so the more I was treated as if I was too much to handle, the more I began to fly off the handle.

When I first made it to the group home I remember feeling like an abandoned orphan, and I had made up in my mind to act like a complete fool. I decided that if my family couldn't control me, the people at the group home didn't have a chance to gain my cooperation. I went in cutting loose on a regular, and the more they tried to discipline me, the more I carried on as if I didn't have a care in the world. I refused to be tamed and it didn't matter how many tactics and mind games they tried to run on me, I was in there on a guarantee to give them a run for their money.

I didn't take it serious at all, and it became like second nature for me to get away with what I wanted, whenever I wanted. I found a way to get around the counselors, and did everything opposite of what they expected. I did not consider that the set rules applied to me. I continued to disobey without regards of the circumstance, and feeling like I could come and go as my mood pleased, I broke curfew without thinking beyond what I had in mind at the current moment.

A few times, I was able to cut in and out as smooth as butter, but when I got caught there was definitely a price to pay. Even though I would always go back to the group home, the staff took serious offense to my casual disappearing acts. It wasn't like I was trying to escape, I would just get the urge to hang out with some of my friends from the neighborhood. I didn't take advantage of it very often, but every once in a while when we got a chance to get some fresh air, I would skip out on an extended break. Unfortunately, group home leaders weren't very tolerable with my sudden impulses to hang out on the block, and considering that I was away without permission, I would face disciplinary actions for being AWOL.

The group home was structured to operate off of a promotion and reward system, which means that I was getting demoted and restricted as fast as I advanced. For the most part my punishments were bearable because I really didn't care about being denied free time and I wasn't that interested in going on any of their field trips. However, as soon as I realized that I was only hurting myself, because my father signed a contract that enforced me to remain in the group home until I successfully completed their instructed course, I decided to fall in line.

It took a year and a half, but I finally had gotten, whipped into shape. Once my conduct exceeded itself to the level of graduation I was, released to go back and live with my grandmother. Graduating from the group home felt good because not only did it bring out the best in me, but it also helped me to rethink my "bad girl" persona. For the first time in a long time, I genuinely wanted to do better. I wanted to re-connect with that little girl who did her best to make every one happy and proud.

When I returned to my grandmothers' house, I was off to a good start. I stayed out of the way, did what I was told, and I listened to what she had to say without rolling my eyes and talking under my breath. I also made sure to stay on top of my chores, so that she wouldn't have to fuss or complain. In addition to that, even though it was a stretch to the outer worlds, I decided to show some respect to my grandfathers' rotten ass.

I still didn't understand why she had to be so strict, but I didn't put up a fight. I just figured that her rules were her rules, and for the sake of not causing any problems, I simply obeyed. I was a different child than the hell raiser that caused her mounds of problems, before she had sent away to live with my dad. Therefore, in my efforts to make things easier, it was my intentions to show her that I was totally, not the same.

Not wanting to face the consequences of veering off task, when it was time to go back to school, I went with a positive attitude and eager to do my best. Do not get me wrong, I still didn't care for being at school that much, I just knew that I had to go. I also knew that I was expected to be a good student overall. In knowing that, I was determined to keep myself going in the right directions. I made certain to do my homework, I didn't have to be told twice to stop talking in the classroom, and I most definitely wasn't trying to be associated with any trouble that would've had me sent to the Principals Office.

Thankfully, the year turned out to be successful, but it was mainly due to the assistance of a very stern teacher, who took time to lean on me harder than Joe Clark. To us students, she was known as Ms. Larry. She was absolutely one of my favorite teachers because she recognized my ability to excel, and pushed me until I was able to see it for myself. She would always talk to me, and tell me how intelligent I was. She also encouraged me to trust that I could achieve anything that I set my mind to. She was a wonderful woman who gave me the confidence to believe in myself, and she even managed to help me get my grades high enough for the honor roll, which was great because I was tired of pretending that my report card had mysteriously gotten lost, on the way to my grandmothers' house.

I maintained a high level of interest for school by involving myself in various extra-curricular activities, and participating in a few literary contests that were available for me to be apart of. I was like the all around girl who went from entering essay and poetry writing contests, to being on the drill team, to running track, and playing basketball. You name it, I did it, and I loved being apart of so many teams. I also loved being able to show off my accomplishments. It was the first time in a long time that I had actually earned some bragging rights for myself, and no matter what place I landed, every win was a big deal to me.

My social life at this point was a little better than the earlier years, and even though I associated with a few females, I can honestly mention that there was only one girl that I considered to be, a true friend. Her name was Jasmine, and I knew that she lived in the   neighborhood, but due to my grandmothers' lock down regulations, we really didn't get to know each other until we hooked up at school. We were in the same class and we hit it off right away. It was like we had known each other for a lifetime, and we were able to relate in so many areas that it was almost scary.

Jasmine was a skinny girl with long hair that she usually wore in two pony tails, platted down each side of her head with colorful barrettes nearly falling off from the ends. She didn't dress fancy, but she always looked clean and neat, and she had a contagious smile with a squeaky voice that sounded like it could almost shatter a glass when she laughed. She had a pleasant spirit about her, but like me, she would often drift off to a distant place in the midst of a full room, and I could recognize that pain anywhere.

I was grateful to have Jasmine as my friend because not only were we able to laugh and play together, but she was someone that I felt comfortable talking to. I knew that I could confide in her without being, judged. I didn't have to be skeptical about letting her into my life because she wasn't the type of individual to hurt anyone by using their own misfortunes against them. I was also confident in knowing that she would never distribute my conversation like free press. She too, knew that I was someone she could confide in, and felt just as comfortable talking to me as well, because most of the time we shared the same frustrations, and cried the same tears.

Outside of school, Jasmine and I were able to spend some time together, but we didn't get to hang out as much because my grandmother would not let go of the grip that kept me locked in the house. She claimed that I was still "too young to be running through the neighborhood", and she needed to keep a close eye on me. Luckily for me, my grandmother was also fond of Jasmine, and she was one of the selected few that my grandmother allowed to come over to visit me. Most of the time when we weren't sitting on the porch talking we were watching videos, and trying to learn all the dance routines while pretending to be whoever had the hottest song at the time.

Throughout the course of our friendship, Jasmine and I became very close, and to me she began to be like more of a sister then a friend. It just eased a lot of tension to have someone who could share the similar heartaches, and understand the turbulent effects of family brokenness, while at the same time helping me to not, feel as if I was alone. I can't say that she was the sister I never had, because indeed I had a sister. I just didn't get to spend that much time with her. Nor will I say that having Jasmine around took the place of my real sister, but it sure did fill some of the voids of not being able to have my real sister around all of the time.

My real sister was my mothers' second child, and it turned out that when she was born, my mother was still committed to her life on the streets, and she was in no condition, to take care of yet, another child. Like me, someone had to step in to make sure that my sister would be properly cared for, and besides the fact that my grandmother didn't have any room, she was really too tired to take care of more grandchildren. Fortunately, there was another family, who did not mind stepping in to help raise my sister. The downside to that was the fact that the circumstances of that arrangement forced my sister, and I to grow up in two different households, and live two separate lives.

Suffering from the same loss of not having our biological mother, my sister and I didn't actually get to know each other until we got older, and she would come over to spend the weekends at our grandmothers' house. We would always have a great time with each other, and though our personalities were clearly different, it was obvious that we were clearly, connected from one in the same.

I loved being able to talk and play games with her. She, in turn loved for us to write songs and perform as if we were superstars. She would play the diva role, and I was the wild child. She loved the front line attention, and I didn't mind shifting towards the background, because once it was time for her to leave, all that mattered was the time we had together. I loved to see my sister come, but it was hard to say good-bye, and we made a pact that we would never allow our children to experience the same pain.

I truly admired my sister, and I held on to the significance of her warm presence even when she was away. I guess that's why I felt so close to Jasmine, because like Jasmine, my sister also had a pleasant spirit, and a smile that could light up any room. That's why, even though my life seemed to have shuffled me around too much to become attached to anyone, Jasmine took up a special place in my heart. I also believe that that's why it hurt me so deeply when Jasmine's grandmother passed away, and during the summer right before our first year of middle school, she was sent to live with her dad and his family somewhere in Florida.

When Jasmine moved, I cried my heart out for days, and I didn't know what I was going to do, without my best friend. She was my sister from another mother, and now that she was gone away, who was I going to talk to about the strange things that I had to deal with in my grandmothers' house. Who was I going to listen to my fearful encounters and tell me that it would be okay, whenever the man I was raised to know as my grandfather decided that he wanted to invade my privacy. Who was I going to cry to when I needed to express the frustrations of being beaten by my grandmother, even though I was trying my best to make her proud. Who was going to relate to the yearning of wanting to be with a mother that would rather lose herself between the cracks of the streets instead of doing whatever it took to stop her family from falling apart. There was so much going on in my life and in my mind that I never trusted to tell anyone else, and now that the one person I felt comfortable talking to had been taken away from me, I was once again, left to face all the drama on my own.

My life as a pre-teen was going through a rapid fire of challenges, and there was no one around me that I could honestly vent my dilemmas' to. Eventually, my frustrations built up to be too much for me to contain, and I began to bleed my emotions onto the pages of an empty notebook that I used as my diary/journal. It was a way to release the issues that were steadily pushing me over the edge, into an area of anger that I knew would not be beneficial for me. As well, it allowed me to confront the situations that were too harmful to reveal on the account that it would have exposed more devastation within a family that was already breading destruction. On the other hand, it helped me to face facts that were too damaging to hide due to the torment that began to deteriorate my motivation to look towards a brighter future.

Working wonders for my mental and emotional stability, writing everything down on paper went far beyond another form of expression. It soothed me in a way that was therapeutic to the soul. This turned out to be a method of self-healing that prevented me from literally losing my sanity in an environment that I thought, was totally insane. I couldn't explain how, but there was something about being able to freely pour my heart out onto those pages that made me feel really calm, and peaceful. It also was a big help with me keeping my composure during the many times that I wanted to just snap, crackle, and pop, because whatever I felt like I needed to get off my chest I wrote in the notebook.

My journal had become my new best friend, and I found myself keeping a log on things that I once would only feel comfortable talking to Jasmine about. Like, how often I would catch my grandfather looking through the gaps of the bathroom door, while I was in the bathtub, and how he would sometimes rub across my butt when I walked past him in the house. I also wrote down how my grandmothers' overtime was wearing her out and making her cranky, causing her to treat me as if I got on her last nerve. I wrote down the fantasies that I would often have about my mother getting herself together for the sake of bringing her family together. I wrote down the concerns I had about being in middle school, and even though I got along with a lot of people, there were still plenty of chatty cats who made it known that they, for whatever reason, just didn't like me.

Pleasantly, there were some few, far, and in between things going on in my life that I enjoyed keeping track of. But between my grandparents, seventh grade and peer pressure, I was so busy focusing to stay in the right frame of mind, that I overlooked what was right in front of me. At least that was the way it appeared because one day I caught a glimpse of myself in the mirror, and while starring at my body in a state of shock, I noticed that I had breast and booty popping out of me like Orville.

Through eyes of amazement, I could hardly recognize the little girl who had started to develop into a young woman, and all I can remember thinking was "WOW! Neffe, you are not going to be the ugly duckling anymore". This meant that I was growing up. It also meant that I didn't need to be hanging around looking like a tom boy, wearing jeans and tennis shoes all of the time. On top of that, it meant that I needed to find someone who I could pattern a sense of style after. This phase of my life was new to me, so I was clueless when it came to accentuating my lady lumps, and the only woman that I was around enough to pay any attention to, looked like she hadn't seen sexy since the sixties.

In the mean time, school was going, though it wasn't going very well because I had fallen off a bit from the previous year. My behavior managed to still be on task, but I wasn't trying to be apart of nothing more than what I had to. I think I must have left my study habits back in elementary. I had yet to get use to so many classes, and all of the work that each teacher would pile on each, and every night. Besides, at this point I was more interested in what the other girls were wearing to class, more than anything the teacher said in it.

Not only was I studying what they had on, but I was also watching how they walked and listening to how they talked as well. I wasn't trying to be like any of them, and I definitely wasn't looking to gain any friends. I just wanted to learn more about the ins and outs of the many different styles and fashion. I would try to find out where some of the girls shopped, and I picked up a few tips on how to wear my hair, because clearly this was not the era to be walking around with my grandmothers' horribly famous helmet waves.

I wasn't getting much from the girls in my homeroom, because like me, it seemed as though they were still trying to figure it all out. Obviously, my maturity extended beyond my immediate classmate sightings, and I was looking towards other females around school to assist me with grasping a mental concept of what growing into a young woman, was about. To my dissatisfaction, I didn't see much to look up to, until one day a distinctive image stood out from the rest of the slim pickings, and I began to observe her from afar.

She was beautiful, with dark skin, brown eyes, and her curvy "coke bottle" molded shape, stood about 5'6 at 135 pounds. She dressed very trendy for the times, and although her hair wasn't much longer than my own, it wasn't likely for her to be caught having a "bad hair day". She held her head high and walked with a confidence that was admired by many, but envied by most and at first glance, I became intrigued by her persona. Her name was Mia, and the more I paid attention to her, I knew that she was the perfect person for me to model after.

Mia didn't know it, but she was a great source of inspiration for me during this period of my life, and though I had no intentions on approaching her, I continued to photocopy her style. We were not in any of the same scheduled classes, but I knew of her from our frequent passes through the halls. I would also see her after school, whenever we ended up riding the same bus into the downtown transfer station. That's where everyone would switch off to head in different directions.

Keeping my distance, I studied Mia like a book and I couldn't wait to get to my grandmothers' house, so that I could close the bedroom door, and review my version of Mia's gesture and poise. I wouldn't say that I wanted to be just like her, but I sure did try to mimic various details that I noticed her doing as our paths crossed throughout the day. I would stand in front of the full sized mirror that hooked onto the back of the closet door and practice that I could mentally recall. The way she walked, the way she motioned her hands when she talked, and the way that she neatly shined her lips, (I substituted Vaseline for lip gloss).

Day after day, I would get home and go through the same routine. I would practice my smile, play in my hair, check to see if my butt had gotten any bigger, and when I wasn't poking out my breasts, I was pushing them together, so that I could make them look as though they had grown a cup size or two. The time I spent discovering myself was a great confidence booster, and it kept me occupied for hours. I was experiencing the fun of my new developments while growing into a young woman. What I didn't know, was that I was not the only one discovering me.

It just so happened that my grandfather was also having a good time experiencing me, while catching an up close and personal peak of my enhancing developments. I went from being uncomfortable to scared as hell, and without letting it be known that I noticed him looking through the skeleton key hole, on the door, I quickly got myself ready for bed. I wasn't sleepy, but my grandmother was at work and I didn't know what else to do at that moment. I definitely didn't want to bring any unnecessary attention to the situation before she came home.

When my grandmother came in, she was in another one of her overworked funks, and I didn't know what I was going to say. I even considered if it would be a wise idea for me to tell her or not. Unable to figure out what I was going to do, I tossed and turned restlessly in the bed, and watched the door through the night. Once I got up to start the next morning, I decided to hold back on going to my grandmother about what had taken place, and I carried on through the day as if nothing ever happened.

A couple of days later, I waited for my grandfather to make his occasional store run, and I mustered up the nerve to go to my grandmother about what he had been doing. I wanted to let her know how uncomfortable it made me, to know that her husband had been using me for his personal peep show, and how inappropriate I felt it to be. I don't know what type of response I was expecting, but before I knew it my grandmother was yelling and cussing me out at the top of her lungs. She told me that she couldn't believe I had come to her with such an absurd accusation. She also went on to say, that my thinking process was off. She blamed it on the fact that I was going through puberty, and suggested that my hormones had me "smelling myself".

My grandmother then added that the only thing inappropriate going on in her house was the way I trotted around like a little hussy. She badgered the hell out of me for at least 30 minutes while I sat quietly on the family room sofa, and listened to her go on and on and on about how I was starting to look like a slut. She continued to downgrade me, and then went on to state that she wondered where I was picking up such bad habits. After a while, I didn't know what was coming out of her mouth because to me she was sounding like a blundering idiot. Somewhere between her opening and closing remarks, the respect that I held for my grandmothers' household, once again, shot out the window faster than a bullet in a drive by.

All this time my grandmother had been isolating me from the outside world, acting as if she was concerned with my well being. I wasn't allowed to do anything, because to her, everything posed a threatening problem. She didn't allow me to spend much time outside because of the dangers that lurked through the neighborhood. She didn't allow me to go to sleepovers because anything was liable to happen to me in someone else's house. Nor did she allow me to visit my friends, because God only knows what type of sin those "heathen children" might have tried to introduce me to.

My grandmother kept me on a leash that didn't extend beyond her front and back yard because she claimed to be so worried about me. Telling me how she was only looking out for my best interest, and making sure that I was okay. When what she didn't know was that everything she called herself protecting me from, had access to me within the walls of her own home. I was hurt, but I was more so angry and I could not believe it. Yet, no matter how I tried to convince myself that it wasn't so, it was really happening. My grandmother took her wounded grandchild, and scared her once more.

I don't think my grandmother ever told my grandfather about our talk, but it didn't matter because from that point on, I cared as much about the two of them as they seemed to have cared about me. I didn't see any use in trying to do the right thing anymore, and the good girl image that I had been portraying went immediately bad. Something triggered in me and feeling underappreciated, I renewed my screw whoever and whatever attitude, and I was dead set on a mission to do just that. I was going to give my grandparents hell to deal with because I was more than angry, I was furious. I didn't give a fuck about my grandmothers' rules. I didn't give a fuck about trying to do the right thing. I just didn't give a fuck, and with all of the catty chats I had to deal with at school, I was wishing for the day for one of them to step up to me the wrong way because I was anxious to beat somebody straight the fuck down.

It was inevitably obvious to everyone around me I was going through a physical change, but with their eyes blocked by the routine hustle and bustle of each day, no one noticed the transformation that was developing from the core of me. On the outside, I maintained a composure that went along with protocol, but in the inside, I was like a Tasmanian Devil waiting on the right opportunity to tear some shit up. I had so much resentment boiling over, that I could feel the heat penetrating every inch of me, and venting on a few pages in a notebook just wasn't going to cut it anymore. Ready to strike out with rage, I could barely contain myself, and hate marked the target from my soul beaten cries.

I couldn't stand being in my grandmothers' house and the more I thought about all the bullshit I had to put up with while living there, made me think that surely my life could not have been any worse off if I was living with my mother. This mess was ridiculous, and if this was the type of screwed up circumstances that she was raised in, then how could anyone blame her for being on the streets. I had already felt as though I just didn't fit in, and now I was feeling like I was absolutely not wanted in the hell hole that my grandmother called, her "home sweet home".

That was no fucking home sweet home. It was more like a bitter bite in the ass, a fiery pit, or better yet, the devils play pin. The longer I had to stay there the stronger I felt the urge to escape that muthafucka, with no return. I wanted to withdraw myself into another shell of secluded misery, but with time moving faster and me getting older, I needed to plot on a way out. Keeping my communication to a minimum, I spent most of my time watching my back from the "peeping tom" grandfather, and formulating a plan for freedom.

All the while, gearing up to be the hell raiser that had been "reformed" during my extended stint at the group home, I reverted back to the stubborn wild fire, that no one could control. I started smoking, drinking, stealing, skipping school and some mo' rowdy shit, on top of everything I was doing to get sent to the group home. I was determined to incorporate a new meaning to my grandmothers' formulated opinion of inappropriate by showing her exactly what was going on right in front of her "horse blinded" eyes.

She had refused to come face to face with the corruption that was breeding within her own walls, and the cold part about it is, what she didn't know was that her house was the one stop shop to all that she had formally forbidden. In her quest to provide the best she could, I'm almost certain that my grandmother had no idea of the fact that she provided the exceptional resources to all that she stressed, and forewarned me not to take part in. The drugs, the alcohol, and right down to the perverted men she tried to protect me from, she made them all accessible for my invaluable use.

CHAPTER 3

PRODUCT OF MY ENVIRONMENT

The Cure

More and more and more I witness as the youth are dying
Because the youth that sprouted them life
Became tired of trying
More and more and more
Are many circumstances growing complicated
Because the sacrifice to teach the youth
Has been dis-associated
More and more and more
Does the struggle seem for those that plead for a way to be free'd
From the image of society
More and more and more
Does the population of homelessness grow
Because wealth is prejudice to the ignorance of don't know, don't have, and
gave up
More and more and more I pray for the foundation of each day
That it may be set on Holy grounds that the floods won't wash away
That the outlook of society would take a deeper look at itself
That the judgers that mock others would see the truth in themselves
That the complainer would look and see that their suffering is not alone
And the best things are taken for granted due to the lack of an un-united
home
More and more I watch as more of our young ladies roam without a clue
Too strong to hear their weakness and too bright to listen outside their views
More and more and more I weep as the young men sprout without the
nurturing to rise
Growing away from the bloom of their maturity never taught to compromise
Never shown by a man how to stand as tall as a man can
And never giving a chance to be steered in a direction
Steel hearted to the warmth of any hand
More and more and more I witness babies killing babies
Or parents never giving a chance to be more than just babies
The more I watch the more I grow
The more I learn that my life is nearly not my whole concern…S.W.

I was like a stallion, bucking to run loose, and one of the first of my grandmothers' rules that I set out to break, was smoking. I started with weed and although I had never thought about getting high before, I was tired of dealing with the stresses that had my mind going in so many different directions. One day when I came home from school, a voice spoke out in my head suggesting that, "it wouldn't hurt to try". With a little more convincing from my own thoughts mixed with boredom, I figured "why not". My grandmother was at work, and I knew that most nights she usually wouldn't make it in until I was in the bed, and as for my grandfather, well I spent most of my time avoiding his old, nasty ass anyway.

Once I decided to go ahead with what I was thinking, I came up with a game plan for how I was going to get the weed, and where I was going to smoke it to make sure I wouldn't raise any questions as to what I was doing. I knew that getting a hold of the weed was not going to be a problem, but getting it without being noticed by my prowling grandfather was my concern. That's when I decided that it would be best for me to wait until he was wrapped up into one of his porno flicks, before I attempted to act out on my newly thought up idea.

Sure enough, within two hours of me being in the house, my grandfather lit a joint, grabbed a beer, and plopped back in the recliner to watch his daily freak show. Giving me the perfect opportunity to make my move, I snuck into the backyard and pulled off a few leaves from my grandfathers' garden of marijuana bushes. He had been growing the plants for as long as I could remember, so I pretty much knew how to break the weed down. I had been watching him do it for quite some time. Being familiar with the process, I knew how to sniff out the strongest leaves, use a shoebox lid to separate the fruit from the buds, and I was like an expert when it came to twisting up a snug zig zag. One in which I happened to swipe out of my grandfathers' nightstand.

Knowing that I could get a hold of the "Sticky Icky", easier than a full course meal, I rolled up a joint, and disappeared behind the shed of my grandmothers' house, in order to make sure that I would remain undetected. When I took the first hit I was caught off guard, by an unexpected choke. It scared me nearly to death because out of all the year's, that I had been around, while my grandfather was smoking, I had never heard him let out even the slightest cough. I remember wondering if I was about to die, because I couldn't catch a breath. I'm sure that if I would have gotten a chance to see my face, I would have died almost instantly from laughter.

There I was with nobody to save me, covering up my mouth so that I could muffle the noise from my choking. I was definitely not trying to let anybody catch me. All I could think was "Oh God", while tears were running from my bulging eyes. It actually felt like my eyes were almost out of socket, sticking half way out of my head. I wasn't keeping track of the time, so I don't know how long I was out there trying to catch my breath, looking like I swallowed a hair ball or something, but what I can tell you is that once I did recompose myself, I still had that joint in my hand. As I Wiped, the wetness away from my eyes and off my face, I couldn't help but to laugh at myself. After I regained my vision and was able to take a deep breath, I decided to cop an "Indian Style" squat in the grass. Leaning my back against the shed, I accepted the realization that I wasn't as much of an expert when it came to smoking, as I was when it came to rolling it up. Of course I was not deterred from taking my second hit, and thanked God that it went much smoother than the first.

Truthfully, I doubt if my grandfather ever got wind that I was pinching out of his crop, or any one else for that matter. He grew and smoked marijuana in such a heavy rotation that he seemed to always walk around with an everlasting high. He smoked in the morning, he smoked in he afternoon, he smoked in the evening, and because he was basically living off of my grandmother, he smoked just about every other hour in between. Honestly, I may not even fill up all ten fingers, if I counted out how many days that he didn't coast along the friendly skies on cloud nine.

In fact, my grandfather would get so high that it would sometimes look like he was on Mars, and one night in particular, I do believe his planet ape looking ass was really trying to get there. It was another evening, when my grandmother was working overtime, and I had just come in from hanging out around the shed, so even though I was in the room lying down, I wasn't quite ready for bed. Next thing I know, my grandfather had come busting through the bedroom door with my grandmothers' red dining room table cloth tied around his neck. I was at a loss for words, because I didn't know what was going on in his mind. All I could think, while he stood in front of me looking like a dehydrated superhero was that he was out of his fucking mind. I swear, if I would not have seen it for myself, no one could have ever told me it was so. This muthafucka was wearing a pair of black trouser socks, and a red cape over his ashy body, with a big dry ass jerry curl, that looked like it was in more shock than I was.

I just knew my grandfather had lost his mind that night, and the more he got to talking about "come see this", as if stark naked standing there with his dick swinging and balls hanging wasn't enough. I was in too much disbelief to not see than crazy ass man was about to do next. He told me to come with him into the backyard, so that he could show me that he knew how to fly, and that's when I knew this shit was about to get even funnier. When we got out there, this man and all his fried brain cells went over to climb one of the poles that held up my grandmothers T shaped clothes line, jumped his feathery ass straight into the air, and crashed landed on his face in a single bound. What he didn't know was that I was just as high as he was and when he took that leap, I fell to the ground as fast as he did. We were both rolling around the backyard in tears, because he hit the ground like a brick, and I was right behind him cracking the fuck up.

Thinking back on what happened the last time I went to my grandmother regarding what I considered to be, an inappropriate act concerning my grandfather, I decided that it was in my best interest to remain silent. I figured that all involved would be better off, if what took place that night was retained between my grandfather and myself, so with never a word spoken, I concealed the incident as a fragment of my imagination. Apparently, my grandfather felt the exact same way, because even though it was a night that neither one of us would ever forget, it was also a night that neither one of us would bring up outside of our own memory and thoughts.

Shortly after I began smoking, my drinking habit made its introductory debut, and just like the marijuana, it was a household necessity stemmed from someone else's excessive demand that provided my overflow. Clueless to the resourceful contribution, this time it was my grandmother that served as the accessorizing party, and thanks to her "Friday night, just got paid" get-togethers, she supplied me without measure. Drinking, smoking, dancing, and playing cards until the break of dawn or until an argument broke out. Which was the signal for my grandmother to send everybody on their, merry little way. It was an anticipated gathering that always seemed to transform my grandmothers' house into a Juke Joint/ After Hour spot, and with people scattered from the front to the back door, looking after grandchildren was the last thing on her mind.

Leaving any children in the house to tend to their own for the evening, we were simply told to get somewhere, other than where the grown folks were at, which usually meant one of the bedrooms. I guess the grown folks wanted to feel free to have a good time and carry on, without children being in their faces. I would go to the bedroom and play games, listen to music, or find other ways to keep myself busy until I fell asleep. Of course, that was before I spawned into the grandchild from hell. Little did anyone know that at this point, I was watching through the cracks of the door waiting to crash the scene.

Though I'd have to admit that watching while the adults freely did their thing was very entertaining, I tried my best to be out of sight and out of mind long enough for everyone to get pissy drunk. I made sure to stay well out of the way, while I listened out for the signal of slurring speech, deafening conversations, top of the lung off key singing, and the arguing with no point at all to kick in, so that I could freely do me. Besides, by this time, even if I was seen, I would be just another blur in the room.

Purposely guided by my curiosity, I would linger around in search of another form of entertainment, and I already had in mind what it was going to be. It was in a Gin and Tonic Water mixed drink that my grandmother referred to as Mr. Boston, and carried through the house in a red plastic cup. Locating it was never difficult because she kept it closer to her than my grandfather but trying to catch it out of her hands was where my challenge came in, because she would hold on to it like a best friend forever. In fact, I do believe that my grandmother spent more time mixing up that drink then she did mixing and mingling with her friends.

Spinning off into a crash course of Alcoholism 101, Mr. Boston taught me real quick, why it wasn't a good idea to guzzle down liquor. It was one of those drinks that had the potential to sneak up on you if you didn't take it in carefully, and the first time I got a hold of it, I gulped it down so fast that it sent me crawling away a bit queasy and light headed. I remember feeling like I had burned a hole in my esophagus, and once I made it to the room, trying to get into the bed was just too much, so I lied on the floor and prayed that someone could turn off the ringing sound in my head. I won't say that the experience was as mind boggling as my initial encounter with the ever stimulating "Mary Jane", but it sure did leave a lasting impression.

Too young to understand that I was not just picking up after my grandmothers' pattern of drinking, but I was in actuality picking up her drinking problem. It took an increasing blow of events for me to even pay attention to the effects that alcohol could have on a person. That may be because as a child, I thought grown folks were all together crazy as hell, so I was unaware of how much alcohol contributed to their irrational behavior. As a matter of fact, I was so use to my grandmothers' get up, go to work, come home, have a drink, and get up the next day to do it all again, ritual, that it never even dawned on me that drinking could even be a bad habit. I suppose that I must have figured a few drinks to be a normal way of life, and if it had not begun to, increasingly affect me in ways beyond my own consumption, I would have never guessed it to be so damaging.

It took me to experience a couple of character conflicts of my own, for me to clearly comprehend exactly how alcohol, and its effects had been impacting my life, well before my curious intake. Up until then, I had never thought twice about the peculiar way my grandmothers' personality shifted every time she sat down to fellowship with her ever faithful, Mr. Boston. Again, I just thought she was a crazy ass old woman, but now that I was putting two and two together, I was able to recognize that my mother wasn't the only one with a sickness that affected our family. I was also able to gain insight for some of the reasoning behind my grandmothers' up rising attacks towards me. That's when I came to the conclusion that frustrated conduct was not solely due to my acts of disobedience, but rather edged on by her amounting stress in conjunction with heavy drinking.

Having to deal with my grandfathers' random disappearing acts, upon many other life challenging frustrations, I truly believe that my grandmother was trying to exempt the burdens that were building up, to break her down. It was around this time, that I realized that drinking was her way of coping with the various disappointments that she didn't want to face head on. The only thing about that form of self healing was that, as soon as the liquor kicked in and got to influencing her to release her anger out on someone else, time after time, that someone was me. As a result, her dependency always left me to feel unjustly punished, and even though I may have earned a couple of those beat downs from actions beyond her knowing. I didn't like the fact that she was striking me; out of her own inflictions and wounds.

Every once in a while, I think that my grandmother even felt like she was unjustly taking her frustrations out on me, because in her round a bout way to remedy the situation, she started giving me an allowance. Like clock work on countless occasions, she would catch me before I walked out of the house for school, and with a shameful "I'm sorry" smirk, she would fold fifty cents into the palm of my hands. Adding fuel to the fire she always followed up with a pat on the shoulder, a speech about how important it was for me to get a good education, and a word of encouragement to "have a great day at school". I always viewed the gesture as nothing more than a guilt trip, and despite the fact that she handed me the measly fifty cents, while stating that it was my allowance, I knew that it was her attempt to exchange sugar for shit.

Trading off as more of an insult to my intelligence than a peace offering, I found it to be quite odd that it never crossed my grandmothers' mind to give me an "allowance", until the mornings after she had knocked me upside my head, during one of her drunken out breaks. Needless to say, that this made me even more resentful towards her and further strengthening the reasons behind my rebellious nature, the only thing her act of kindness encouraged me to do, was get into more shit. Like stealing for instance, because that's exactly what I started to do once she decided to smooth over her brutal attacks by buying her way into forgiveness with change that only enticed me to want more. I can almost bet my life, that she had no idea that her notion to keep me content activated a notion within me, to turn her coin purse into my no hassle banking service.

Impulsively developing another home instituted habit, I began using my grandmothers' oval shaped change purse to unzip unlimited access to her funds. She was my personal savings, and I made certain that she provided my needs unsparingly. Every time she cashed her check, I didn't hesitate to make an unaccountable withdrawal. After a while, I was taking money out of her bedroom dresser drawer, pants pockets, and wherever else I suspected her stash to be stored. Without shame, I began to take whatever I could find, wherever I could find it, and when she would question me about any missing cash, I transformed into the box of rocks she always played me to be, and drew and unsuspecting blank. Not sure of where to point the blame, she would spurt out comments around the house like "I could have sworn I had more money than this", and knowing his mode of conduct, I would respond back by suggesting that, "maybe granddad needed some of it".

Another thing my grandmother wasn't aware of, was that when she called herself patting me on the back, and sending me on my way to "have a great day at school", school was not apart of the agenda. Most of the time my intentions to have a great day at school had nothing to do with me even being there. Unless I was showing up to stay long enough to not be counted, as absent on my attendance record. At this stage, my mind was restless and school was turning out to be as nerve wrecking as my grandmothers' house. With the pressure of both places weighing down on me, I was always looking for an alternative destination. I would leave out of the house as if I were on my way to school, but in actuality

I was in route to search out a place where I could go, and not feel like I was in a hostage situation, or boot camp.

My confidence was elevating into new highs, because I realized that I was able to get away with skipping school just as easy as I had been getting away with stealing alcohol and money from my grandmother, and weed from my grandfather. I guess I figured that since I was getting away with so much, there was no need to hold back from trying to get away with more. I upgraded my thieving tactics from my grandmothers' house to corner stores. I adapted a motto of "why spend what you don't have to". So even when I had the money I got a kick out of exercising my right to the five finger discount, until one day my sticky fingers got my ass in a sticky situation. It just so happened to be that one day while I was stealing out of the same corner store that I had been hitting up at least three times a week, the clerk caught hold of me, and all of my boldness. Proving the theory that criminals can make some of the dumbest mistakes in the world. That's when the police drove me, and one of my cousins who happened to be with me at the time, to my grandmothers' house. That's when she exercised her right to kick our ass.

Obviously not thinking, I made matters even worse for myself by attempting to out smart my grandmother, by stuffing toilet paper in the back of my pants while my cousin was getting his beat down. Once it was my turn and my grandmother realized that her hits were not affecting me the way she thought they should, she snatched me up and quickly noticed what I had done to relieve some of the pain from her back to back blows. The idea didn't pan out exactly the way I played it in mind. Boiling her over into a new extreme, my grandmother made sure that I felt all of her frustration. Beating me like never before, she stepped on my neck, put a chair over the upper portion of my body, sat on it to secure that I could not move, and wore me out.

Still not learning my lesson, that beating didn't do anything, but confirm the fact that my grandmother was insane. At this point, with me beginning to challenge her authority, it was as if everyday brought about a head on collision, between two head strong, tyrants. No longer attempting to hide my unruly behavior, I was being outright rebellious, and with her attempt to keep me in order, she was being straight up abusive. I continued to be disrespectful by keeping up everything that I had got into over the course of the previous few months, and she continued to tear into my not so sunny side up. I would get caught stealing, and she would catch my naked ass in the bathtub with an extension cord. She would find out that I had been skipping school, and she would try to confine me to the house. Even thought it didn't make a bit of a difference because I would sneak out the back door, as if she was motioning her lips on mute.

I knew that somewhere deep inside of me, I loved my Nanna, but it was time for all of that bullshit to come to an end. I was getting older, my life was growing tougher, my sense of placement was all together offset, and though she had been raising me from the time I was a baby, I was angry with her. Mentally, I wasn't able to comprehend that she just wanted to protect me, so I didn't appreciate her position in my life. I had not considered the efforts that she had been putting forth to take care of me while in her household, and at the same time, she wasn't taking the time to understand that I had been longing for a bond she couldn't mend. The friction among us escalated into a knock down, drag out fight that nearly drove me out of my mind, as her increased rages of frustration, clashed with my lack of obedience. Ultimately, I knew then that sooner than later something was going to have to give.

In the mean time, I couldn't escape the connection that burdened the depths of my soul, and my desire to receive that irreplaceable love of a mother, began to weigh heavier on my heart. Chocking me up through a constant attack, my individuality faced doubts, and wrestled with a confusion that overwhelmed my mind, causing my emotions to cry out for understanding through a rigorously brewed rebelliousness. That's when I made the decision to no longer be complacent with my life the way it had been handed, and came to the conclusion that the best thing for me to do was leave. I realized that a lot of the pain in my life was caused by a lot of unanswered questions, and the only way for me to find happiness was to find the only person who could fill in the answers.

I wanted to know where my mother was. I wanted to hunt her down, and ask her why she had not come back to rescue me after so many years of being away. I wanted to hear her tell me what was so important on the streets that she wouldn't even make time for me. Then I wanted to let her know that I forgave her, and that I needed her in my life. It didn't matter that just about everyone around me tried to make her out to be some type of disease. She was my mother, and in my mind, I was going to find her, so that together we could make everything alright. I was on a mission to bridge the gaps and bring my immediate family together, while my grandmother had her mind set to do whatever it took to make sure that I would not follow in my mothers' foot steps. I truly believed that I was strong enough to help my mother lead and support a foundation for us as a family. However, it turned out that my agenda conceived, only to show just how much my mother and I had in common.

It wasn't like the thought of an escape was a new idea, in fact it had been crossing my mind day after day for quite some time, but I had never built up enough courage to see it through on my own. I would always change my mind at the last minute thinking that every strategy that I had come up with was never the right one. Over time the constant backing out added more stress to my frustrations, because even with revising my plot to run away on a daily basis, I couldn't figure out why I remained stuck. Then it dawned on me that the reason I had never left, was because I had no idea where I could go. Out of all the time that I had been spending, contemplating a way to get a way, I had never thought through a sure plan of what I was going to do once I actually got away. The one for sure thing that I knew was that every nerving moment at my grandmothers' house stirred up a thicker resentment. Now that I had received the revelation as to "why", I was unable to flee from the Brookfield Dungeon I was even more determined to come up with a successful plot for freedom.

At this point, I began to dedicate most of my energy to finding a way out, and in order to make sure that I had enough planning time to scheme I went from ditching school two to three times a week, to about three or four. I began to roam the skip circuit with some of the other students who felt like school was nothing more than a waste of time, hoping that I could intuitively catch on to some of their street savvy ways. To no avail, the only thing that I can honestly recall picking up, while following those characters was the need to not, feel like a misfit.

Thinking back, this was also the time that I caught wind of the nicotine trend. This just so happened to be one of the few habits that I could not link back to my grandmothers' house. I only wish that I could tell you that I picked up my first cigarette to sooth and relax my thought during the strenuous moments. In fact, I can't even associate it with my own self will, because the truth of the matter is that the only reason I started smoking cigarettes, was to show that I was as cool as the crew that I called myself keeping up with. Later in life I learned that this was just an inadvertent attempt to latch on to the feeling of acceptance that I longed for.

Passing over into the next couple of weeks, I still had not come up with a solid plan for my escape. Considering the increasing urgency of the situation, I knew that my time to get away was counting down to desperation. I was tired of being squeezed between the belittling issues that were brought about by my family, and the pressures to be respected for who I was at school. Though I had been showcasing a role of resilience, I felt as if I was being wrung out to a dry death. Not to mention that my mind was persistent with convincing me that living with my mom could not possibly be as bad as everyone made it out to be, and with that being noted, giving up on my mission to break loose was not an option.

One day all of my Colt 45 guzzling, cigarette smoking and shit talking paid off, when I unexpectedly ran into one of my home girls from the neighborhood. Her name was Toya, and she grew up around the corner from my grandmothers' house. Like myself, she also had a mother who was battling drug addiction, but unlike my situation her mother didn't turn her over to dysfunctional grandparents. For a moment, I had been wondering what was going on and why I had not seen her, because our paths had not crossed in quite some time, so when she approached me it was a pleasant surprise. I was excited to see her, because she was more than just another girl on the block that I knew, but someone that I was able to relate to.

Toya and I were very familiar with the hardships that one another had been dealing with over the years, so talking to her was like listening to my own voice, outside of my own head. Normally, whenever we spent time together, we would end up having a lengthy and in depth conversation, where no one else seemed to exist beyond our talkative bubble. So being that we were on the side of a local liquor store during school hours didn't make a difference in the world. The deeper we got into our discussion, I began to share with her my desire to get from under my grandmothers' claw's, and with a slight grin, she told me that she had something important to let me in on.

Toya went on to explain that the reason I had not seen her around the neighborhood was because she had ran away from home. Right then, I became all ears as she continued to talk about how she had been able to survive on the streets for nearly four months before her mother caught up with her. The more she went on the faster my heart raced with the excitement of just thinking over the possibilities, and once she confessed that she was gearing up to run away again, I became charged by a refreshing encouragement.

Ironically, I was able to recognize that this was an opportunity of a life time, and I became too anxious to let it pass me by. I broke out of my quietness to let Toya know, that I wanted to be apart of her next departure. I didn't even care to hear the details at that point. The only thing that mattered to me was the fact that I needed a way out, and Toya was going to provide it. Besides, there was no up front reason to not trust her, and knowing that she had already accomplished what I had only been dreaming to make happen, was more than enough for me.

Looking at Toya as an angel sent to my rescue, I poured out my heart until tears spilled out of my eyes, and she comforted me with a hug while telling me that she knew of a place where we could go. That statement was like a relief to my soul and all of a sudden, everything cloudy became clear. I was ready to take flight, as my concerns for safety evaporated into thin air. Personally, my thoughts suggested that there was nothing to lose and everything to gain. So of course, it never dawned on me that I was about to twilight zone into a new form of hell. I guess my vision didn't peek beyond the familiar realities that our lives entangled, and to me it was more of a miracle than a coincidence that our paths crossed during my acceding desperation for escape.

When it came time for Toya to head home for the day, we finished off the pint size bottle of Wild Irish Rose and agreed that she would call me that evening, so that we could come up with a concrete strategy to leave. After she left, I decided that it would be a good idea for me to head to my grandmothers' house, so that I could prepare for our departure. I figured that there was no time to waste, and I wanted to have my things together, so that I would be able to make move with ease. Once I got up to the front door, I heard my grandmother talking on the phone, and she seemed to be a bit upset. Initially, I was shocked to even hear her voice, because it was unusual for her to be home from work so early, but at that moment the horse I was riding stood so tall, that I didn't give it a second thought.

Walking into the house without saying a word, I strutted right past my grandmother, and gave her a look as if I was untouchable, while she sat on the couch, chewing somebody's head off through the phone. Consumed by the thoughts of knowing that I was going to finally run away, it slipped my mind that I was wearing one of my grandmothers' outfits, and without a warning, as I headed towards the bathroom she slapped me upside the back of my head. Smacking me back into the real world, she yelled at me for taking clothes out of her closet. Incidentally, due to the fact, that this was something she would get on me about, quite often I was immediately, dealt with. Threatening that I had better not show my face, my grandmother sent me to the bedroom and told me to think about my actions. At that point, the only actions that I had planned to think about, was the ones I was going to take to get the hell out of her house.

Crossing over into the evening, that night climaxed into a finale that I would never forget as I bluntly ignored the punishment my grandmother called herself putting me on. My mind was pre-set to defy her instructions, because Toya and I had arranged to discuss our plan to run away. I wasn't about to let anything get in my way. Unconcerned with the consequences,

I sat near the bedroom door, and listened out for the phone to ring. In the mean time my grandmother, dozed in and out on the couch, while waiting for my grandfather to come in.

Finally, the phone rang, and I snuck out of the room to answer it, only to hear my grandmother yell out for me to get off the phone. Actually, "Get the fuck off of my phone", were her exact words. Even though I knew that I heard her, I carried on with my conversation, as if she wasn't speaking to me. "Neffe if you don't get off the phone, I'm going to beat the shit out of you!" she yelled out once more. This time to make it clear that she was absolutely talking to me she picked up the other house phone, and screamed in my ear. As the fury raged in her voice, I hung up the phone, eased back into the bedroom, waited about five minutes, and slid my way to the phone once again, so that I could call Toya back.

Once my grandmother realized that I was on the phone again, she began to yell out again, and just like before, I defiantly did just the opposite. In fact, as I think back, I can clearly remember telling Toya that it was crucial for me to leave, and insisted that she meet up with me right away. She agreed, and we decided that which ever one of us got away first, would wait for the other, in the field that was located next to my grandmothers' house. I suggested the field, because even if my grandmother noticed that I was gone, she would not have suspected me to be in what she considered the trash lot. It was like half the size of a football field and basically invisible to her, with only a few scattered trees, there were more empty beer bottles, cigarette butts, syringes, and other debris covering the ground than grass. Besides, I figured that if nothing else we could blend in with the junkies and winos that aimlessly slugged around.

While finalizing the game plan, I could hear my grandmother coming closer, as she continued to yell for me to get off the phone. Then all of a sudden, I felt an unpleasant stinging sensation across the middle of my back. Instantly, I realized that my grandmother had come up with her own game plan for me. Indeed, she was not playing when she told me that she was going to beat the shit out of me, and as I began to swell up from the big ass orange cord that landed repeatedly on my flesh, all

I could think was, "This is the last time I'm going to let this bitch hit me". I'm telling you as soon as she finished beating me I was like fuck it, and my motivation to leave was ignited by the determination to never return.

My grandmother didn't stop beating me until she was nearly out of breath. Then she told me to get ready for bed, and warned that if she so much heard a peep out of me for the rest of the evening, she was going to make me wish that I wasn't alive. I wanted to tell her that I had been dead for years, but I just looked at her and said "Yes ma'am". Starring at me, as if she was about to rip my head off, her eyes followed me all the way into the bathroom, not knowing that it would be the last time in a long time, that she would lay eyes on me.

I wasn't in the bathtub long, because the whelps over my ass, stung like hell from the water, and when I came out of the bathroom, I noticed that my grandmother was on the couch knocked out. She must have used all of her energy to beat the shit out of me, and worn herself out, which worked out great for me, because I was gearing up to make a fast break. After I got dressed and grabbed a few items of clothing to put in my small blue tote, I went into my grandmothers' bedroom and took everything that she had in her little change purse. Then I walked softly towards the door, and gave my sound asleep grandmother the middle finger, as I left out of the house.

When I made it to the field, I felt a sense of relief to see that Toya was already there waiting on me, and after a quick hug she asked me if I was okay, as we headed for the bus stop. Hopping on the first bus that showed up, I didn't know where we were going, and I didn't ask any questions. I was just so grateful to be away from the house of doom. It was late, so the bus was fairly empty and after riding for about ten minutes in silence, Toya looked at me with a compassionate expression. Once more, she assured me that we were not going to have anything to worry about. At this point, I had already put my life in her hands until I was able to locate my mother and strike out on my own. I could only hope, wish, and pray, that what she said was real.

We rode the bus to the downtown area of Oakland, where we got off to make a transfer. That's when I finally decided to ask Toya where we were on our way to. That's also when she told me about the pimp who had been taking care of her while she was on the streets, before her mother found her. Immediately, I froze up, and with a slight feeling of disappointment, I explained to her, that after being raped I had no intentions on being a recruit for prostitution. Not judging her for what she chose to do in order to survive, I was able to clarify my point, and we came to a common understanding, that it would be best for me to head in a different direction.

Watching Toya ride off on her next bus was like watching my future fade into the darkness of night. The cold part about it was that I was standing there with no idea of how to bring it back. I wasn't sure what I was about to do, or where I was about to go, but I definitely knew what was absolutely not an option, and that was going back to my grandmothers' house. After, Toya was long out of sight, I decided to get on another bus, and ride until I could sort things out in my mind. It didn't matter which bus it was, or where it was going. I just needed some time to figure out what my next move was about to be.

Trying to fight back the tears and gather myself, I sat at one of the bus stops, and out of nowhere I heard someone say "excuse me, don't I know you from school?". When I looked up to see who it was, I saw Mia, the girl that I had taken on as my sergeant role model, standing to the left of me. Shocked, that she even noticed who I was, I responded yes. From there she went on to question my reason for being out so late, looking as if I was lost. That's when I made a formal introduction, and opened up to her about what happened to me that evening.

Looking as though she felt sorry for me, Mia invited me to come and stay the night at her house. She went on to let me know that the house would be crowded, and that she hoped I didn't mind sleeping on the couch. Of course, in my mind I was jumping up and down, because before she showed up, I just knew that I was about to be sleeping on somebody's park bench. I asked if she was sure her mother would be okay with me popping up at their house unannounced, and she assured me that it would be no problem.

When we arrived at the house, Mia introduced me to her mother and once I went over my story with her, she got up from the kitchen table, walked over to me and gave me a nice long hug. I hadn't had a hug like that in a while and it felt good. It made me feel as if she really cared. With no further questions asked, Mias' mother looked me in the eyes and called me her little black sapphire, and welcomed me into their home. Initially, I didn't really know how to take the fact that she was so receptive to me so quickly, but as I allowed myself to relax, I began to feel like I actually belonged.

Mia's mother went on to tell me that I could stay as long as I needed. In her efforts to help me understand that she could relate to what I was going through, she also went on to talk to me about the fact that she too, was a run away. She opened up to me about the story of her childhood, and how even though her mother wasn't using any drugs, she was extremely abusive. She also let me know that, just because she was letting me stay there didn't mean that I was free to do as I wanted, and she did not expect for me to drop out of school. Not in a position to debate, that's when I realized that like my grandmother, she strongly believed that education was the only sure way out of the mess that held us captive in a fabricated ghetto.

I went to sleep that night feeling so grateful, and to make certain that I honored my word to Mia's mother I got up the next morning and went right to school. I went into my first class and stayed long enough to be accounted for on the attendance record, and left school grounds immediately after. I was thankful that I had a place where I could rest my head peacefully, but I wasn't forgetting that my main purpose for leaving my grandmothers' house in the first place, was to find my mother.

Mia knew the mission that I was on, so she never threatened to tell her mother what I was up to, and some days she would even hit the streets with me. After about three weeks, I began to realize that there were not enough hours in the day to find my mother, and I started to sneak out of the house when I knew everyone was asleep. That didn't last long at all before Mia's mother found out and warned me that if it were to happen again, she was going to have to put me out. Needless to say that it happened again, and holding up to her word, Mia's mother sent me on my way.

At this point, I wasn't afraid to take the risks of being on the streets alone, because I just wanted to find my mother. Even if took me to the streets of Oakland. However, I didn't know that the course ahead would strip me of just about all that I had to give, plus some things I had no idea I was even capable of giving. It was a cold exchange as my mentality transfigured into a whole new awareness. While I conveniently said good-bye to pride, dignity, integrity, and my self- respect. I had entered into a pool of ruthlessness and numbness sedated my sense of being as the streets released an inner personality that combated manipulation to survive. I found myself all up in the mix and the traps but, I wanted to be with my mother, and that's what came with the territory.

Clinging to the edge of existence and searching for my safe-haven, I had finally allowed my brave heart the opportunity to showcase its unquestionable loyalty. I knew what I wanted, I knew who I was looking for, I knew there was no turning back, and at that time, I thought I knew enough to manage on my own. I know it sounds crazy as hell, but I held a love for my mother that could not be explained, and if her lifestyle couldn't accommodate me I was determined to take on her lifestyle. I felt like I could take on anything, and nothing was going to hinder what I had set out to do.

CHAPTER 4

IN NEED OF A MOTHERS LOVE

BITS AND PIECES

In it to win it
Losing everything I had
Knowledge what?
Integrity who?
Pick your trick out the bag
I cashed in for a loop
Spiraling beneath surfaced winds
Rode a long way with insidious intentions nearly met my end
Courageous I raged to be
Could handle any curve turning
Until I saw it was me
Before I knew it
Before I knew it
I was all I never expected to be
Acting out of regional composure
Far into the defects of maturity
Carrying on into the middle of my self destruction
Overtaken
Overwhelmed
I was in mid air
Dropped from nowhere
With no pleasant landings below
Betrayed by the excitement of flash by exertion
Crossed me for a sudden blow
What I lived for was death
What I died for was killing me
What I thought I'd never become
Is what my main attraction showed at every entry…S.W.

Believe me when I tell you that it's a proven fact that the Lord looks out for fools and babies, because I was fresh out the womb of an ass. Seriously, I have to laugh, while I sit back today, and think about how brave I was, as I made my way through every crack and crevice. I was a young girl maneuvering through increasing demands of iniquity, and the search for my mother, as I confronted a multitude of ho's, and pleaded with numerous pimps, wrenched me like a damsel in distress.

I would love to tell you that I found her shortly after I made the big get away, but the reality of that fairytale is not so. Truthfully, I lingered back and forth between Mia's house and the streets for nearly two years before I actually made contact with my mother, and the bullshit that I had to endure just to rest my neck from one day to the next was demoralizing. The more crap I encountered the clearer it became that I escaped my grandmothers abuse only to open myself up for every kiss of death that shot out from life's sudden blows.

My views of survival had taken a twist, and I had to conform through whatever form of misuse rolled my way. I was no longer a little girl, but fresh meat ready for slaughter as every snake eyed pervert, crook, and pimp that Yaya fought so desperately to protect me from, side betted a claim toward my misfortune. I rummaged through the days with no idea of how long it would take to find my mother, as each moment became a passing gamble that I relentlessly did what deemed necessary to get by. I felt as thought I was already without everything I had to lose, so instead of going back to my grandmothers' house I mentally equipped myself to entertain the game for what it played out to be. Instinctively, I learned how to depend on using the streets just the same as the brood vipers that preyed upon my innocence, attempted to use me.

During this time of my life, I adopted the concept that "A fair exchange is no robbery", as apart of my daily routine, while I loosely allowed just about anything to go down. I wasn't clueless to the fact that many helping hands only reached out to help themselves take advantage of me, nor was I a blind sighted victim. I was a thirteen year old runaway operating with an emotional wall that certified my durability to be resilient. I walked the streets asking around for my mother in the day and by night I had the luxury of choosing between giving a muthafucka head or sleeping in the park. It was a mode that insinuated my leverage of survival to include all, but standing on the corner for pick up.

Most of the time I would meet someone throughout the day, and by the time night came around, I would have talked up on a place to sleep. I found that method to work out pretty convenient for a while, and if I ever went home with a nigga who wanted to send me out on the strip for his personal grind piece, I would just leave and never go back. Usually, the guys were straight up like, "if you don't have any money, then you need to suck my dick or let me fuck you", that didn't bother me as much, so I did what I felt like I had to do. I guess, I figured that was one of the only safe ways for me to make it through the night.

Unfortunately, I found that not to be the case one evening, when I attempted to express the fact that I wasn't interested in exchanging sex for a place to sleep. I simply tried to explain to a nigga that turned out to be crazy, that I was out looking for my mother, and that the only thing I needed was somewhere to rest, so that I could continue my search the next day. Responding as if he understood and respected where I was coming from, he gave me a T-shirt and a pair of shorts that I could sleep in, handed me a blanket and a pillow, then pointed me to the couch that I was to sleep on. Lying down with a sigh of relief, I was just grateful that he didn't give me a hassle about not wanting to fuck and all that other bullshit, the other nigga's expected me to do, in order to rest my head.

Tired from all of the walking I had done earlier that day, I fell asleep within the matter of minutes, but it wasn't long before I was disrupted by a rude awakening. I can't tell you what time of the morning it was, but all I know is that I was woke up out of my sleep by a heavy handed slap to the face and pulled up off of that couch by my neck. I tried to fight back, but my strength was no match for the three men, who nearly beat me unconscious, blind folded me, tied me to the kitchen sink, and took turns raping me with no remorse. I promise, I wasn't expecting the nigga to be crazy, and as my thoughts replayed the first time I got raped, the only thing that I could do while the tears ran down my face, was hope that the horrible moment would end soon.

Once they finished with me, my mind was in such disarray that I could hardly make sense of anything that was going on, and next thing I know is that I was being thrown outside. I was in so much pain and I had no idea what I was about to do. I was ashamed to go back to Mia's, because her mother had already stressed for me to slow down, and warned me of the dangers that I was bound to run into. I had too much pride to go back to hear the "I told you so" and the "that's what the fuck you get", speech from my grandmother, so I convinced myself that if I was able to get past the first rape, I could survive what had just taken place.

Picking myself up from the dirt, I made my way to the nearest gas station, so that I could clean myself off, and prepare myself to continue my search as if what had happened never did. Eventually my risky endeavors of dodging pimps and fighting off cut throat, nigga's was as common as the sun rising to set. One way or another, I intended on tracking down the woman who birthed me. At this rate, I didn't care what it was going to take, and even though it nearly took my life, I still didn't consider backing down from wanting to be with my mother.

Learning the hard way, showed me how mandatory it was for me to incorporate a guarded approach, as I struggled to avoid the bread winning stroll along the ruthless trenches of International Blvd, known formally as East 14th Street. This scenic jungle love of death through deception was a Ho Stroll that had a reputation of tricking out more consumers than Cross Colors. Thriving from the bright lights that flashed in between the trash where the prostitutes showcased their ass for a sack, a dime, and/or some cash. It was a strip entanglement where the pussy had the power, but the dollar ruled the crown. It was a home where the players unsparingly played, the hustlers got paid, and what you had could get you glad or turned the fuck around. It was a way of life where the only limit was green, the only way to cut corners was getting laid, and the only way to do dirt was without a soul surviving sound.

I was a teenager, but I comprehended that there was some serious shit going on, and with the intensity of weariness weighing in, I couldn't afford to fall off slipping. I treaded with my eyes wide open and my antennas finely tuned, so that I could catch everything that crossed my path, because I knew the consequences of taking what was going on around me for granted. I also knew that it was a free ride to hell in a trap of destitution, and not only did I watch, but I was all caught up fighting against the flat line while spinning into my demise. Accelerating me through a new dimension of living where my sense of direction, lead me into a world with no sense of humor. I'm telling you there was nothing to joke about on those streets, and the instant you cracked a smile, was the instant you were liable to be cracked in the fucking head.

Increasingly, the road that I had been traveling was breaking me down to just about nothing, and having nothing to turn back to, there was nothing else for me to do but to continue pushing ahead, so that's what I did. My common sense, maintained my very low tolerance for bullshit. The anxiousness of finding my mother was built up to an all time high, because just like my previous moment of grieving desperation, I knew that sooner than later something had to give. I didn't know what, I didn't know how, and I didn't know when, all I knew was that I had to be getting closer to some sort of relief.

The next couple of days, I continued to hope, wish, and pray, while carrying myself through the streets. The routine was like frustrating intervals that drug me through a roller coaster of disappointments, from asking questions and receiving no concrete answers. I was weary, but determined, and I beat the streets endlessly, until one day, I linked up with someone who would turn out to be the man that changed my perspective on life, forever. Offering me a priceless relationship that ended up being somewhat of a ghetto love story, the next monumental transition of my life began something like this:

"What's your work out here little momma?"

Here we go again, another day, another pimp, another frustrated moment to let it be known that I didn't want to be bothered with another smooth runner, stopping me on some ole' sharp tongue bullshit.

"I'm not out here to sell my body and I'm not looking for anybody to put me on the market." I responded, with a projected aggravation to discourage any further questioning.

"What's your name?"

" I ain't no ho!" I snapped viciously.
"What the fuck you want?"

"Look here, I ain't trying to strap you up, I'm just asking your name."

"My name is Neffeteria." I answered

"Yo' momma named Frankie?", he replied.
   What the….The very second I heard her name broke me down but I knew that any sign of weakness could get me killed and I didn't know who this man was or what his motives were with me.

"Yeah, who are you?" I cocked back, with a combative stance of composure.

"Get in the car I know exactly where your mother is." Spoken with a firm security his words hit my heart like a sudden rain in a drought.

"Are you serious?" I shot out earnestly blank as I tried to rationalize my mind with a round of questions I really wanted to know.

How did this man know who I was? Or better yet, how did he know my mother? As the conversation went on, he explained to me that when my mother found out I had ran away from home she sent people on the streets to look for me the same way I was looking for her. Surely, you can just imagine how skeptical I was, as I stood there like a statue staring at a man who popped up like a jack in the box, claiming that he knew "exactly" where my mother was, and the cold part about it is, I trusted him.

I trusted him, even though I knew how much danger that my life could be in, and I let my guards down, because at that point of my life, I just needed someone to believe in. I was at a very low place, and I needed this to be the milestone that generated a lifeline to pull me from the tyrannized journey, that the streets had shuffled me through. I needed him to be the one man, who was willing to help me get to my mother without a hidden agenda. I needed this to be that divine connection to reuniting me with my mother, so I got in.

Strapping myself in for the ride, released a confidence that I had not felt in a long while, as my insides buckled from a sense of relief. Purposely cutting our conversation short, I didn't want to show that I was comfortable, but just the thought of my days, and nights, and months over a year, of burrowing along cracks, corners, and crevices coming to an end, excited me beyond words. Once again, God had sent another Angel to rescue me and this time it wasn't my friend from around the corner, but someone that knew my mother, who had met me on the corner where he was known as Mac Truck.

Indeed, Mac Truck was telling me the truth and the excitement that surged through me once I seen my mothers' face, left me speechless. Through the tears, we could barely take our eyes off of each other as we admired the presence of one another through the eyes of unconditional love, faith, and forgiveness. This reunion had been "A long time coming", but the goal was accomplished, and my mother and I were together, and our immediate connection sparked an emotional outbreak. All of a sudden, nothing about our past was strong enough to overshadow that mother/daughter moment, and every struggle that I endured to arrive at this moment, delivered its promise.

It was a moment where containing the tears was impossible, because I had traveled a broad distance, in and out of some severe conditions, because I needed my mother. It was a moment where I reached out for the only woman who could validate my sense of being, to embrace her wounded child. It was a moment where I couldn't hold strong even if I wanted to, because I needed to hear my mother tell me that she loved me and at that moment, she did. For the first time that I could remember, my mother held me in her arms and told me that she loved me, and for the first time, I was able to say to her the same.

"We are family!" Hey, it was time to celebrate and upon no conventional terms, we had us a reunion within our own little isolated "I got my momma and me" world. It was a joyous occasion as we marveled over experiences from our street wars and horror stories. In the exchange of our bliss, things sure did liven up as we continued, shared a bite to eat, a nice joint, a few drinks and more personal glories. We had a ball. We talked through a reminiscent era of "back in the day", while the harmonic tunes of our laughter and cries strolled us even further "Back down memory lane". In that moment time commanded a stillness that allowed our time apart to catch up and we vowed to never separate from each other again.

Again, I was able to enjoy a moment that I had been so desperately seeking for nearly two years. It was a moment that I wished could never end, but unfortunately I was the only one who felt that way, because before I could get in good, my mother was ready to get out and get her next high. Leaving me to feel disappointed once more, my mother flipped the script on me faster than road runner, and the only thing that I could do was wonder what the hell was wrong with her, while I waited for her to come back.

Once the excitement of being reunited with my mother faded behind the scenes of her outreached reality, the real work of our striving togetherness kicked in like Desert Storm. I felt like I was in the constant line of fire of a never ending battle, as my mother stayed into everything, I pleaded her to stay out of. Clearly, her control had been granted a furlough well before I made my infantry arrival, and trying to get her to come together as a unit, was like trying to block a mid-day sun ray in the Sahara, with no hint of shade. Her lifestyle forced us to live from pillar to post, meaning that just about everyday we were in different dope houses, trap houses, hotels, and wherever else she could secure a hit, along with a place for us to rest our heads.

My mother had us relaying along ruthless grounds, where everywhere was a land mine, and her method of movement was censored through a strategic motion. She wasn't just out to get by, but to get over on any muthafucka who was flimsy enough to get knocked off of his game. As the days went on, I began to consider that my time on the streets was more like basic training, compared to the actual war zone that accompanied my mothers "I'll fuck you over, if you let me" tactics. To make matters even worse every effort I put forth to keep up with her had me dizzier than a sit and spin. Before I knew it, I went from fighting just to survive, to beating up women more than twice my age, cursing out pimps, hustling over hustlers and anything else that I can't think of right now, all for the sake of my mothers thrill to get high.

My mothers habit of choice was not available without a price, and watching her suffer the cost from a high that continually bound her to every low that life had to offer, tore me apart. I felt powerless as she insisted on wearing herself out on streets tailor made for destruction. I felt helpless as she patched up old scars with a temporary fix from suppliers that never had enough to give and never got enough of what she had to offer of herself. I felt unhappy as I saw my mother drape grief with strung out lies while garments of restlessness covered her remorse.

Once more I suppressed an eruption as I concealed another suffocating pain into the depth of my soul while I witnessed my mother casually fade away. In my eyes it wasn't worth it as she repeatedly sold herself out to an addiction that blind sighted her true responsibilities for a fulfillment of false hope. Right in front of my eyes, my mothers self inflicted infirmities hijacked her identity and robbed her of the very life she struggled to hold on too. It was a devastating overturn as I watched my mother barely cope, wishing that she could see herself through the eyes of me.

No matter what she had been labeled in my eyes she was my mother. Far beyond the years of gridlock she had been buried beneath, she was my mother. When I looked at her, I seen a woman I had longed to be with all of my life. I didn't see a junkie, or a prostitute, or whatever else her lifestyle may have branded. What I seen was a woman who had been drug through the mud and still standing clean. I seen her recovered, not from using drugs but from being used by them as she neurotically endured the abuse. She was without a blemish as I looked from the core of my heart and seen my mother for who she was and not who she appeared to be.

For what it was worth, I seen my mother as a precious jewel worthy of so much more than the venomous society she wanted so much of. I seen her living a life much greater than any pipe dream could ever promise, because I seen her through the eyes of God. Even then I had enough spiritual understanding to know that our Heavenly Father has a purpose for us all and He sees us for who He created us to be. I also understood that I shared an instinctive connection with my mother too un-natural for the carnal mind to ever know or conceive.

I couldn't explain the bond that drew me away from home, trudging me through an agonizing melting pot of wretchedness but I knew it was strong and so it did. It was like an eternal mandate beyond the universal ethics of life evoking me to believe in my mother when no one else wanted to, but I knew somebody had to and so I did. I was her first born and I had been allocated to initiate the first step in exploiting myself on a quest to secure the future of our family coming together as a whole. I carried enough faith to take on the expedition of finding my mother because I knew that all she needed was little help from somebody who would vigorously maintain by her side.

I held enough faith to genuinely cover my mothers' hell grieved flesh through the infernal deprivation that thrived over her ingeniousness, because I knew that the true light of our Heavenly Father would set her free, in a time of His own. I knew that even though the path she pursued clouded any sight of defection, it would be just a matter of time before the manifestation of her weaned horizons, blazed a trail to map out higher standards for the following generation to uphold.

In the mean time, I had unofficially delegated myself to take charge and lead the way. I knew that my mother was performing the best she was capable of at the time, but she was clearly unable to sustain the stability we needed to maintain. Living on the streets like a chicken with my head cut off, while I was looking for my mother was one thing, but now that we were together the life of aimlessly roaming was truly for the birds. We revolved within a cluster of cut throats, with rules as cunning as the games being played. It was an environment where the treacheries heeded an astute keenness as not to get crossed out of existence. So while I continued to trust and pray that God's plan for our lives would come to pass, I began to contemplate a plan of my own.

Patterning former methods for survival, I conservatively scoped over a wide range of prospects in a scenic scenario, where many of the same circulated perpetually amongst themselves. Through an assessment of previewed targets within the secluded arena I conjured up a prominent approach and positioned myself to stake claim. It wasn't an innovative idea but a reliable one as I locked in on a hunch for execution. Rating my contingency ratio highly attainable over not, this was a bet I was willing to turn over my life for, and I did.

On the streets, he was known as Mac Truck and when our paths first crossed on the strip, all I saw was another pimp trying to round up a trollop for his collection. Stopping just short of violation, I veered off into a defensive rampage explicitly expressing that I was not available for anybody's pick up. Even still as I acknowledged his presence to be Heaven sent, it took me some time to recognize his potential role in my immediate future. I was so deep into my self perseverance I couldn't decipher his capabilities to cancel out every want and need that professed a struggle in my life.

Surprisingly, the situation revised itself as our acquaintance frequently meshed in the midst of anything goes, and in countless measures he carried the traits that I had been scouting for. He was a stand up character, captured pleasantly in a quaint disposition with essential accreditations placing him as a fore runner against all odds. It took me a minute, but I began to take notice, that right before my eyes, in plain distant sight was everything that I could hope for.

He was a stellar individual with a swagger that announced his slender built structure and well groomed distinctiveness on arrival. He went by a creed that translated cut swift, and shoot without a chase, and everyone knew to give him 50 feet. He embodied high respect for others and stayed to himself, but he was territorial, and warned that others should tend to their business, so that he could mind his own. His temper was like an engine, meaning that when everything was good, that's what it was, but once shit ran hot, everything shut down with possible costly damages. He was a deep thinker and he believed that all things would work together for the good of all involved, so long as all involved were on the up and up. He was the go to man. He was the watch me make it happen, and get it done proper man. He was the man that rode fly and ranked considerably above the low risers with a quota that bartered no exceptions, and tolerated no excuse. He was the man I needed on my team.

I didn't hesitate to stake the claim, and my assured confidence for success to accomplish the task at hand, was the awareness of knowing exactly what I was up against. I had studied him in passing and due to an accumulation of inevitable circumstances, I knew which cards to lye on the table in order to attract his compassion. I knew that shelled beneath the hard ass portrayed was a vulnerable entity whose sorrowfulness would not allow a young girl (such as myself), to be left unattended in a cruel arena.

I based the extent of my proposition on facts that overpowered the obvious, on top of the facts that I publicly faced. I was sure that if I went to him with the fact that I had never been loved, and for so long the only affection I received were from men who made me suck their dicks, just for a place to sleep. The fact that, even though I was sexually active I never had a man to make love to me, because I had only been used for the ejaculatory advantage, of everyone that ever penetrated me. The fact that I was tired of getting beat down by nigga's and beating up ho's, additional to the facts that I was practically still homeless, still living on the edge, and far from her voyage to recovery, my mother was still out of hand, refusing to slow down for anything or act right for shit. The fact that I knew my life was at the end of its rope, with no string attached dealt some facts that I knew would force his hand to fold.

Again, Mac Truck was in the position to be the extension that my life required in order to me to hold on, but it was just going to take a little time to assist him with grasping the concept, of how much of him that I needed for my life. He also didn't know how determined I was to bridge an attachment between the two of us, and even though he tried to be reluctant, his resistance was no match for my persistence. I was on a mission to create a means of survival for my mother and myself, and rejection was not an option. Therefore, every time he attempted to discipline his actions by telling me "No", I went on to extend myself as if there were "No holds barred".

I expressed the need to receive all that he had to give, by showing him that I had no intentions, on accepting no as his final answer. I knew that he possessed all that was needed to relieve my mother and me from the distress of street wars, and I was not going to let up off of my pursuit. I knew that with him traveled a whole new light of life and I wanted every bit of it, so I seized every opportunity to gain the rights to my claim. I aggressively used what I had learned on the streets to dominate his every intention to not give in, and gradually the efforts of my advancements transmitted a Bull's Eye.

It wasn't an easy land but as he subjected himself to my enticement, I was no longer a commander without a chief, and my relationship with Mac Truck was setting for a new horizon. I was in my first relationship, but more than that I was about to have my first real experience to every great thing a man could be. He was the first man that I had come across who treated me like I was actually worth something. He was the first man who truly cared about me, and when he took me under his wings he showed me life through a projection I could have never imagined, and a hell of a lot more.

Mac Truck did not hold back from showing me all that life had to offer. He made it a priority for me to know that out of all that life had to offer, understanding was the most beneficial. Covering everything that could come to mind, from making love to making money, and what I didn't know he had patience to teach. He taught me the importance of being well rounded, and did whatever he could to make certain that I was equipped to be just that. He made it apart of his business to transition me from a young girl being taken advantage of, to a young woman making her way through the disadvantages of life.

In the streets, he schooled me on how to protect myself with some vital insight on how to spot shit before it released a stench. He also taught me about the dope game and how to pistol whip both bitches and nigga's the same. In the bed, that grown man brought out some emotions in me that I would have never ever guessed existed. I mean, I had been fucking, but I never knew what an orgasm was until Mac Truck made love to me. He wasn't just a good man, but he was good for me, and the fact that he had a wife and two children didn't change a thing. He was my partner, stepping in for every lack as we tagged the barbaric underworld that I had grown to know as a caged rumble to the death.

My relationship with Mac Truck was moving at a rapid pace with a steady flow, until all of a sudden everything came to a complete halt. I couldn't believe it, but as I sat in the back of that police car, I knew it was very real. I had been on the streets for nearly three years, and right when everything was going in the direction I needed it to go, my evil ass grandmother had tracked me down. I was upset, but I also knew that I was considered to be a, 14 year old, run away and I had to go with the authorities.

When I arrived at my grandmothers' house, I was definitely not the same scary 12 year old, adolescent who ran off with a friend a couple of years back. I wasn't the same young girl that wanted to search out her mother for a fresh start at life, but I was now a full blown teenager, who had survived more hardships, than most adults would ever care to admit. Still, things were no different than when I left. My grandmother was still talking shit, my grandfather was still a weed smoking fool, and the tormented pain from years of my stripped innocence, continued to reveal the nature of a cold hearted beast.

Every day I woke up, with a throbbing desire to leave again, and every night I laid down dreading waking up in my grandmothers' house the next morning. All I did was roam around the house and think about the kind of life that I had been abruptly uprooted from and I wanted it back. I thought about my mother and what she was into while I wasn't around to look after her. I thought about my new life with Mac Truck and even though I pursued him to make certain my mother and I would be taken care of, it felt good to have a man who genuinely cared for me. I was accustomed to the way our lives were going and I knew we were building something that I just wasn't ready to give up, so roughly 14 days later I ran away for the second time.

CHAPTER 5

JOURNEY TO CHANGE

NOT THE LOVE FOR ME

Stop it
Please, stop it
I call out to you at the tip of my weakness
In a brutal besiegement
With each second dragging longer than the last
Cease this match
I'm not qualified
But victimized
In defense I reach back
Lash
I'm on the wall
Compact crash
I'm on the floor
I can't breath
I feel paralyzed
My babies are terrified
Weeping helplessly, as they watch
Silent tears drain from swollen eyes
And it's not over yet
I – Can't – Get- A- Way from here
My Lord, You said I should never have fear
Of man
But this man has his hand around my neck
And I'm choking but I can't choke
Is there no sorrow for my hope?...S.W.

Amazingly, when I left my grandmothers' house, I didn't set out to reconnect with the life that I felt called me back into the streets. Instead I routed along the same path that followed, the first time I ran away. I caught the first bus that pulled up, rode it into downtown Oakland transfer station, and waited for the number 82 to arrive, which was the bus I needed to take me to Mia's house. I Knew that it was a gamble, but I showed up at Mia's house in the middle of the night, and begged her mother to let me back in, even though I'm sure she was tired of me coming in and out of her house as if it was my personal safe-haven.

Threatening that it would be the last time, Mia's mother was unable to make her little black sapphire stay on the streets, and as she held the door open for me to walk inside; she cussed me out without a breath in between. The lecture didn't bother me, because I knew she was going to lay me out on sight, so I was mentally ready to digest all that she had to say. Leading me into the kitchen, to look me over, as she continued to chew a new hole in my ass, Mia's mother, placed her arms around me the very same way she did the first time I was invited into her house, and again gave me another welcoming hug.

Expressing my gratitude for sheltering me once more, I told Mia's mother how much I loved her, and that I truly appreciated the fact that she genuinely cared for me. She then looked at me, and went on to voice her concerns about which way my life was headed and warned, that if I didn't slow down, something terribly bad could happen to me. Tears began to run down my face, while I continued to listen in without a word spoken from my mouth. I knew that what she was telling me was real, and not only could it be possible to happen, it did.

Closing off the conversation, Mia's mother went into her bedroom and brought me out a change of clothes, along with a pillow, and a couple of blankets, so that I would be able to rest easy through the night. Unaware of the horrible situation that I had to endure while previously on the streets, she then directed me to the couch, and with a warm smile, told me to get some sleep. I didn't have the courage to tell her what had happened to me, but with flashbacks from the last time I fell asleep on a couch still fresh in my mind, I waited for her to go into the bedroom and curled up on the floor.

The next morning Mia came shoving on me bright and early, so that I could wake up, and with her eyes full of joy, she told me how happy she was to see me. Once I was able to finally make out what she was saying, I realized that she had something exciting to talk about. When I got up, she gave me a wash cloth and towel, so that I could get dressed for the day, and we headed to the mall. The mall was directly across the street from her house, and we would often go there to walk around and discuss what was new in our lives. It was more like our designated spot to talk about everything we had been going through, while pointing out everything we wished we could have.

While making our rounds through each store, and catching up on life from the last time we were together, Mia told me that she had someone for me to meet. As we were leaving out of one of the department stores, we were approached by a muscular built man, who stood about 5'9, with a caramel complexion, and features that were quite tasty to the eyes. Out the gate, I just knew that he was the one that she was talking about, but to my pleasant surprise, it was the guy walking along side him, who Mia introduced me to as, her boyfriend Edmond.

Edmond was also a good looking guy, and when I caught a glimpse of Mia's glowing face, I could tell that he made her very happy. They had been dating for about six months, so she thought she was in love, and as I would soon find out the two of them were rarely ever apart. On the other hand, I had become intrigued by the mysterious fellow, that I learned to know as Rick, and being that he shied away from the forefront, made me want to know even more about him.

Rick was Edmond's Uncle, so he would come by Mia's house frequently, on account of his nephew, which was always a delightful treat for me. He was in his early 30's, and was heavily involved in the dope game. He didn't speak much, but every time he was around, his presence always seemed to give me goose bumps. In fact, I couldn't wait for Edmond to show up because I knew Rick wasn't far behind. I was so infatuated by that man that I would sit and wait by the window and listen out for the music in his car, so that I could watch him pull up in front of the house.

One day out of my infatuation, I built up the nerve to make an approach to Rick and despite Mia being totally against it, I pounced on the opportunity to be with him. He didn't put up much of a fight and that night we ended up kicking it in a hotel somewhere on another side of town. After we hooked up, I was stuck, and he instantly became my personal fantasy. I wanted to have with him what Mia had with Edmond, and even though he let me know that it was impossible, I tried to make it happen anyway.

I used what Mac Truck had taught me, and did everything in my power to show Rick that I could be a great asset to his team. I jumped aboard to help package his dope, make a few pick ups, drop offs, and whatever else that was required to help his business run smooth. But the fact that he had a common law wife with children at home to take care of had me stuck at doing just that. I was so naive at the time, that I wasn't able to see the truth beyond what I wanted. Then again, I suppose that even if I did see, I would not have wanted to accept the reality that I could never be anything more than a shadow, behind a man who already lived behind the scenes.

Though he had put me in the mind of Mac Truck when we first met, Rick turned out to be a totally different character, and the arrangements that we had during the few months that we were together came with a lot of restrictions. There were only a few places we could go together, and only certain people who he allowed to even know that I existed in his life. I was just so happy to be with him that it didn't matter. I guess in my mind, I was thinking that I would eventually win him over.

Soon after we started fucking around, Rick started beating on me. And even though I felt like I didn't deserve to be hit, it still didn't stop me from wanting to be with him. I truly believe that in some weird way, it made me actually want to be with him even more. I can remember plenty of times when Mia wanted to intervene and say something, but Edmond would always threaten her to mind her own damn business, so in tears she was force to listen as I cried out from the pain of Ricks repeated blows.

Rick would feel the need to hit on me for various reasons, and often times, I think he was just frustrated and needed someone to take it out on. Making up any excuse as to why he treated me so awful, he would complain that I wasn't dressed properly, or fuss about how I didn't package the dope right, or anything else that he could think of to smack the shit out of me. He even tried to run me over with his car one day, and that is when I figured out, that he must have been using as much dope as he was pushing out.

Obviously, not knowing the value of my self worth, instead of leaving Ricks crazy ass, for brutally beating me as if I was someone he hated, I tried to kill myself. Only proving that I was just as retarded as he was. I can recall more than one occasion within our short lived fuck and fight relationship, when I slit my wrist, all because I wanted him to love me so bad. I felt like I needed him and once I realized that he had no intentions on taking me serious, I just did not want to live life anymore. Now that I'm thinking about it, I'm wondering what was laced in the weed that I was smoking?

Anyway, things only got worse over time as Rick continued to beat me, and one day while he was going off on me, he received a 911 page. Thinking that it was a big transaction, he called the number back only to find out that Edmond had been killed. It was a time that was hard on both Rick and Mia, with both of them grieving in their own way. Mia burned candles and cried for days in a dark room, while Rick went into seclusion. My mind still didn't understand at the time, so I paged him every hour on the hour for days with no response.

Nearly three weeks went by without me hearing a word from Rick, until one day, he decided to pop up, out of the nowhere. Not knowing that that would be the last time that I would ever see or talk to him again, Rick took me to the hotel so that he could have sex with me. Without warning when we were finished, he beat me senseless. He even drug me down the street, while calling me a young whore, amongst other insulting things. After he got tired of beating me, he took me back up to the hotel room and fucked me again. When he dropped me back off at Mia's house that evening, he didn't even say two words as I got out of his car, and as he drove off, he drove out of my life forever.

During that time, Mia and I were both dealing with heavy hearts, and grieved through the next couple of weeks. I guess while we were grieving, Mia's sister was planning, because a few weeks after our wounds started to heal, Mia's sister told us she had a surprise to show us. She said she would show it to us once we were the only ones at the house. Sure enough when the house was cleared except for us, Mia's sister had us follow her to her room, and she pulled two medium-sized black bags from under her bed. She threw one in each of our arms, and we sat them on the bed to see what was inside. We all counted to three in unison, and then we unzipped the bags. To our surprise, there was money in both of the bags.

Wondering where her sister got the money from, Mia asked her sister about all of the suspicions she had about how her sister got the money. Her sister explained that the money was their grandmother's savings that she kept hid in her house. When I look back on it, we were all dumb as fuck for spending their grandmother's life savings. But at the moment we were very excited and anxious to go and spend most of the money across the street at the mall. We purchased a multitude of clothing and accessories, but the most prized-possession that I bought were a pair of black and white Grant Hill, Fila's.

We walked out of the mall like we were the baddest bitches walking on this planet, with our heads held high and a bus load of bags in our hands. Before we actually made it to their house, we saw what we thought to be a neighborhood friend, but he instantly showed us otherwise. He ordered us to drop all of our merchandise that we had just purchased, and on top of that we were told to empty out everything we had in our pockets. Initially, I thought he was joking because I mean, it was broad fucking daylight, but once again he showed all of us different when he pulled a gun out of his pocket and yelled, "Break Yo' selves Bitches!" I knew then that not only was this nigga very serious, but he was crazy ass hell, and that's when I took off running for help. I got half way down the block and didn't see anyone that I could ask to help us out of the situation. That's when I realized that I wouldn't be able to explain to anyone that knew us how our broke asses got into that type of a jam in the first place. The only thing I could do was think, "damn, this nigga really gone take our shit". I was in a total state of shock, as we handed over everything that we had just purchased, with the money that Mia's sister stole from her grandmother. That's when I quickly found out that, Karma is a muthafucka.

Between Edmonds death, Rick leaving me, and being robbed at gun point in broad daylight by a nigga I actually considered a friend, I was just too through. I figured that I would have better luck on the streets with my mother, so that night instead of staying over Mia's I hopped on the bus and headed to the strip. While I was riding to bus into the heart of Oakland, I replayed everything that I had been through over the previous couple of months and could not help but to consider that my life was doomed to revolve around bullshit.

When I made it to East 14th Street, I ran into Mac Truck within four hours, and we hooked up as if there had been no time lost. Unfortunately, a few months later, while I was 15 the police picked me up. Again, my grandmother had sent the cops to track me down, and for the second time. They took me to where I knew, I was totally out of place.

Things were crazy, and I didn't understand why my grandmother just wouldn't lay off. I was practically grown and with everything I held under my belt of experiences, following rules other than the common street laws were out of the question. As the days dragged on my mind continued to wonder about what I was missing and for the third time I began to plot on getting back to the life I knew suited me best. Unfortunately, my grandmother knew to watch me like a hawk forbidding my every premeditated move.

It was my 16th Birthday and being that the list of Holiday's my grandmother didn't celebrate included Birthday's, I knew not to expect much, if anything at all. I also knew that my chances of getting out of the house was slim to non, because I do believe my grandmother purposely took the day off just to keep a hawks eye over me. As the day clocked into the late afternoon, I had gotten a few "Happy Birthday" calls from different family members and a couple of friends. That alone made me feel grateful, to know that someone other than myself thought of me, on my Birthday.

I was hoping to hear from my mother, but I canceled that thought out almost as instant as it came in. I hadn't heard from her since the police picked me up and brought me back to my grandmothers' house the first time. I also knew that the people in hell would have a better chance at getting ice water, before that woman would take time out from the streets to acknowledge any of her children's birthday. Then I began to think up another far fetched wish and that was, to be able to hear Mac Trucks voice, and entertaining the concept for just a moment, I believed that it would be more likely for me to catch a falling star. I sat and starred out of that front room window for about 45 minutes daydreaming about all of the great experiences that I had been able to share with Mac Truck and how I desperately wanted to be with him. I knew that being with him meant that I wouldn't have to think about celebrating my very special "Sweet 16", because he would have surely showered me to the extreme, at least that's how I imagined it.

Dwindling from my fascination, I continued to relay various thoughts of wishful thinking while watching neighbors and passing traffic through the curtains when out of nowhere an unknown vehicle turned into my grandmothers' driveway. I had no idea who it was and from the first glance I thought it was one of my grandfathers' pot head friends. I couldn't wait to send them away because he wasn't home. As the tinted windows rolled down the driver side of the car, I noticed a man looking around as if he was checking to see if he was at the right house, and that's when I realized it was Mac Truck.

Like always Mac Truck had come to save the day, and I jumped up from the couch with so much excitement, that I nearly fell to my face, tripping over a rug in my grandmothers' family room. I was rushing to the bathroom, so that I could check over myself and make sure that I wasn't looking a mess when I answered the door. He must have been just as anxious to get to me as I was to greet him, because it seemed as though the doorbell rang within in milli-seconds of me seeing him step out of the car.

My grandmother was in her bedroom resting from the night before and I knew that I needed to get to the front door and escort Mac Truck off of the porch before she woke up to find out who had just rung her doorbell. Luckily, she had a hangover and didn't hear the door bell to know that anyone had come by the house, because when I opened up the door, I couldn't get two words out before Mac Truck sounded out a sweetly sensual "Happy Birthday Baby Girl". Literally, my insides bubbled over with joy as I was greeted with a moist cake, a delicious kiss, and a warm sensual Happy Birthday that shot me off like a champagne cork.

Trying not to allow my excitement to overpower my awareness to keep the noise down, I convinced Mac Truck to step around to the side of the house while I tip toed inside to set my gifts in the bedroom. Wearing a smile that wrapped around my head, I remember feeling like I was on top of the world and when I made it back outside to where he was waiting for me I put my arms around his neck and gave him another kiss. Then he told me to follow him to the back of the car and once we made it to the trunk, he looked deep into my eyes and told me that he loved me while handing me the keys. Opening the trunk as he instructed, I was shocked to see that there was a bike inside and as he stood behind me he whispered in my ear another "Happy Birthday", and informed me that both the bike and the car were for me.

I could hardly believe it, Mac Truck had showed up to shower me with one surprise after another, and with each one getting better as he continued to present, I completely forget where I was. I began jumping up and down like I had lost my mind, and shouting "Thank You" and "I Love You" as loud as my vocal cords would let me. I won't say that I was loud enough to awake the dead, but I sure did get my grandmother to rise up out of her coffin, because that's when I heard her loud ass yelling at me from the front porch, "What the fuck is going on out here?" and

"Neffe, who in the hell is that man?".

Responding as if she was the grandchild, I hollered back "This is my man" and "Look what he brought me for my birthday". That's when I believe my grandmother popped a cork of her own, but instead of bubbling over, she went straight the fuck off. She came running out of that house like someone had yelled out "fire", and the next thing I know is that we were going at it like two grown women, while Mac Truck stood sturdy by my side. When she realized that he wasn't backing away, she started an attack on him, by threatening to call the police and stating that he was going to go to jail for statutory rape, and a bunch of other shit that was coming out of her mouth. Giving my grandmother a grin of sarcasm, Mac Truck walked over and got into the car and the more she yelled for him to "Get the fuck away from her house", the more I yelled at her ass. Things were heated and out of control with my grandmother pointing at her front door and yelling "bitch you better get yo' ho ass in the house", and me still refusing to back down while hollering back, "I ain't going nowhere, but with my man". That's when Mac Truck started up the car and told me to calm down and respect my grandmother, and he also assured me that everything was going to be alright. Before he pulled off, he reached out of the car window with a birthday card and as I went to get it out of his hand he once more assured me that things were going to be fine, by telling me that he would be waiting for me later on that night.

Mac Truck disappeared without a trace as my grandmother warned that he should never show his face, around her house again. I was so angry, that I can remember giving my grandmother a look that could have ignited her into an instant spontaneous combustion, and she looked right back at me with the same flaming eyes. She continued to point and yell out "Get your stupid ass in the house", and though she reached for it when I crossed her path, she pulled back from trying to grab the envelope out of my hands, as she watched me hold my birthday card close to my heart.

Going into the house, things were still heated and for whatever reason I went from feeling like a teenager to a full blown adult, and the same way my grandmother continued to cuss at me, I was cussing at her ass right back. We went back and forth as if there was no love between the two of us and as soon as she would say, "Fuck you…" I replied, "Fuck you too…". The more she went on to scream out, "Bitch this…" I hit her with a rebuttal like, "Bitch that…" until my grandmother pulled a set of keys out of her night stand.

The keys went to the barred gates that guarded the house and showing them to me was my grandmothers' way of showing me that what I said didn't matter because my life was in her hands. Our battle simmered down with my grandmother telling me that I was never going to be allowed outside again, and I made it known that I was sure to be a ghost by daybreak. I don't know if she believed me or not, but I was just as serious as she was meaning to be, and as she dangled the keys in my face, she called me one last "ignorant ass bitch". Refusing to allow her to feel as though she had total authority, I voiced back "I hate you" while stomping away. My grandmother and I both went into separate bedrooms and you could hear both doors slam almost simultaneously. I'm not sure what she did once her door was shut, but I fell across the bed and cried my heart out, because I was still hurt about my man being run off.

I buried my head in the pillows that were propped up by my hands and thinking that I would eventually feel better, I cried until I woke up with a hole still in my heart. The hurt of what had taken place earlier continued to weigh heavy on me and as I looked around the room to see my birthday cake, my eyes began to swell with tears once again. Right then, I remembered that I had shoved my birthday card under the pillow before I fell asleep being that I was no longer in the intensity of the situation, I realized that there was something much more than a card sealed inside of the envelope. When I opened it up, I was blew away by another surprise, because even more than the money I expected the birthday card also came with a key and directions for me to get to the house I belonged to. Suddenly the excitement that came along with my "Sweet 16" Birthday revived itself, and I was preparing for my next great escape.

I walked out of the room and through the house to see what was going on, and I noticed that my grandmother was sitting on the couch. She was slouched back in her favorite spot, with her favorite drink and watching television. She too, noticed me as I walked past her, and with a look of disgust she fixated her eyes on the keys that she had on the coffee table that sat in front of her. Looking back at me as if she dared me to touch, I simply starred back at her ass, except that my look wasn't one of disgust, but it was more like, "I bet you wake up tomorrow and I won't be here".

Turning away without saying a word, I walked back into the bedroom thinking about how upset my grandmother was going to be, when she realized that her keys were as useless as the man she referred to as her husband. She wasn't aware of the fact that I didn't need her keys to get out of her house, because my grandfather had figured out a way to unlock the gates, for the purpose of his own personal benefits. I watched him tamper with the locks one night and I caught on as fast as he rigged it, so getting out was no issue, it was getting back in that always gave me a problem.

Taking a deep breath as I sat down on the bed, I grabbed my birthday card and read it over once more. After that, I got up to pick out one change of underwear from my clean cloths basket, and I folded and stuffed them in the right front pocket of the jeans that I had on. Then I walked over to the dresser drawer that held up my small round, white frosted cake, and as I read over it once more, I thought to myself "he didn't forget". My body tingled as I ran my left index finger across the bold red lettering that spelled out "HAPPY BIRTHDAY NEFFE", because knowing that I meant enough to Mac Truck for him to remember my favorite color, meant a lot to me.

I eased myself through the house and to the back door around eleven o'clock p.m. I wasn't concerned about getting caught, because by this time any activity that could go on in the house was at a stand still for the night. My grandmother had drunk herself to sleep, waiting for my grandfather to come home, so she was on the couch comatose. Which left me to look out for my grandfather, and knowing his nasty ass, he was most likely laid up with one of his other women, with no intentions of coming home. Once I made it out of the house, I walked quietly along the side and into the front yard and headed toward the bus stop. When the bus pulled up, I eagerly got on and paid my fare, and I walked to the center of the bus to sit down I felt a sense a freedom that filled my heart with joy. Sighing with relief, I closed my eyes and smiled from the thoughts of knowing that there was someone who truly cared for me.

Following the instructions that Mac Truck had written on my Birthday Card, it didn't take me long to make it to my final destination. I arrived at the house that matched the address on the card and shook the key out of the envelope and into my hand. Then I used that same key and unlocked the door to a place that I knew was for me and I didn't mind calling it "my home". Tears were flowing down my face as I entered the dimly lit house, but this time, rather than crying out from hidden pain, these tears were released from a feeling of unspeakable happiness.

Stopping just beyond the entry way, and I circled the room, and noticed a tall lamp that stood in the corner behind the black leather sectional that was positioned to the right of me, and with my eyes surfing the scenery, I locked in on my man. Mac Truck was sitting back on the couch and with his arms reaching towards me, and his strong voice spoke out "Welcome Home". Instantly, my 16th birthday shifted from gloomy, to grateful, to glorious within in a matter of hours and without going into detail, that night reinforced my crossing over into womanhood.

I got up the next morning while Mac Truck was still asleep and toured the small, but comfortable three bedroom house, that I was excited to claim as my home and Thanked God. I looked through every room, closet, cabinet, and drawer, to see that the house was cozily furnished and stocked with everything that I could ever ask to have in a home, plus some. He also knew that I had developed a love for cooking and supplied my kitchen with everything from a refrigerator full of food to a complete set of dishes, to cook ware, to silver ware, and more, and it was all mines.

Once I finished my walk through I decided that the least I could do was let Mac Truck wake up to some pancakes, sausage, cheese eggs, and grits. While eating breakfast at the kitchen table, I continued to express my gratitude and appreciation for all of the wonderful things that he had done, and with a firm confidence he reassured the statement that he would always be around to take care of me. He then went on to let me know that the house was mines, free of financial obligation and that all he needed for me to do was help out with one of his Uncle's.

I had never met anyone in Mac Trucks family before so, I had no idea who he was talking about, but at this rate, I really didn't have any reason to put up a dispute. Another reason that I accepted the responsibility was because I knew that it was Mac Trucks justified proposition to take care of me, especially, when it came to dealing with his wife and children. He didn't want me to be viewed as a "bitch" off the streets, but someone who could "assist" him with keeping a close eye on an ailing family member.

Further explaining the arrangement, Mac Truck told me that he needed me to make sure that his Uncle, in which I would learn to know as J.M., was properly looked after. The requirements were nothing difficult and basically, I was expected to make sure that J.M. was fed, bathed, and changed on a regular. As he went on to reveal more information to me about J.M., Mack Truck let me know that he was around 48 years old, and that he had been injured three years prior, during a drug deal that went bad on the strip. Continued to tell me the that the injury was near fatal, and that not only did the gun shot wound leave J.M. paralyzed from the waist down, but it also left him bitter and emotionally distressed because of his lack of independence. Mac Truck then added on for me to not be fooled by his Uncles' disability and forewarned me that just because J.M. was wheelchair bound, didn't mean that he wasn't harmless.

When J.M. moved in, he seemed to be a fairly decent man, and he wasn't hard to deal with right from the start, but that didn't mean that I was going to ignore what Mac Truck had told me. I knew that Mac Truck always kept my best interest in mind so whenever he would give me a warning I would take heed, and though I did what I could to make sure that J.M. was comfortable, I stayed very cautious. It didn't take long for me to notice his frequent mood changes, but they didn't bother me because for the most part I knew that I was the one in charge. I guess I had some sympathy for his situation and whenever he would go into one of his "I don't want anyone to help me" and "I don't want anyone around me", phases, I just got the hell out of the way.

Other than that we got along very well, except when he felt like he was getting lonely for a woman and figured that since I was there to cater to his needs, he could catch a free feel to see how available I was, but when I cussed his as out, he bagged the fuck up. Besides, he only tried that type of shit when no one else was around and being that Mac Truck stayed in and out J.M., didn't act like he was too crazy, too often because Mack Truck had the tendencies to get as angry as J.M., and J.M. was aware of that. J.M. also knew that unlike himself Mac Truck still had the ability to put his foot up somebody's ass, rather they could feel it or not.

Though Mac Truck had a wife and children, he would spend a majority of his time with me, and he would only go home to check on the children and feed his wife the dope she needed to stay off of his back. When he wasn't at the house with me or seeing about his family at home, he was making sure that his stocks were properly exchanging on the strip because when his money wasn't right neither was he. As the weeks went on, a transaction that went sour on the strip, sat one of his runners down for a while, and the threat of his investments going belly up forced him to increase his business demands with hands on involvement.

Mac Truck didn't like to run a messy operation and with things getting out of control, he felt the need to personally monitor his market and make sure that what was going on was all that it was suppose to be. That meant that he would be spending less time at the house with me and more time on the streets, and knowing who I was dealing with, I knew that it was important for me to let him know that I understood. I didn't put up a fuss, nor did I interfere with his decision making, I just upheld the position he had placed me in and made sure that all was properly taken care of when he did come around.

Things were going smooth and Mac Truck continued to make sure that I was well taken care of, and being that he didn't want me out hustling in the streets, there was nothing I asked for, that he didn't supply. From clothes, shoes, jewelry, cars, and more, I had just about everything a teenage girl could want and he provided it all, in an effort to keep me comfortable. I seemed to be content with my life, but on the inside I knew that there was one more request that I needed to be fulfilled, and that was finding my mother.

Anticipating Mac Trucks reaction before I even brought up the fact that I wanted my mother to get off the streets and come live with me, I decided to approach him about it anyway. His immediate response going into the discussion was that, he didn't think it was a good idea, but because he loved me and knew that I loved my mother he would find her and bring her to me. He went on to warn me that I would have to watch out for her and that I would also be responsible for fixing whatever problems she may cause while at the house. Once he laid down the law, he asked me if I was certain that looking after my mother was something that I really wanted to do, and I responded with a confident yes.

Two days later Mac Truck came in with my mother and just like many times before, the excitement from the two of us seeing each other overrode everything in between. We stayed up talking and making plans about what the future was going to be like now that neither of us had to wonder how we were going to make it, because Mac Truck was there to cover all of our needs. Continuing with our conversation, my mother had a sudden urge for a fix, but this time she didn't have to run to the streets, because I had just what was needed to keep her sitting still. I guess I figured that if I could supply her needs, she wouldn't have any reason to go out and hustle herself through the streets just to get high.

The days went on and Mac Truck began to put more responsibility on me, and at that point, not only was I keeping and eye on his Uncle, but his wife's drug habit had gotten worse, so I had to help take care of his two children as well. Between running the house and running shit in the streets, I was running into all types of shit. Fortunately, Mac had taught me how to handle it all in stride, so even though it was running it was flowing smooth. Things at times seemed to get a little crazy, but overall it was a good place in my life, and I was able to experience being happy, without wanting for anything, at the same time.

Then all of a sudden, Mac found out that my mother had been pinching out of the stash we had stashed away inside of the house. Forced into a situation, where I had to step up, to block out some bullshit that my mother had gotten herself into, I had to confess to Mac Truck, that I knew momma was sneaking in the dope, but I was hoping she would slow the fuck down. Instantly he went off and told me that since it was my mother I was going to be the one responsible and needed to get out there and make the money back. As the repercussions fell on me, I just envisioned myself choking the shit out of my mothers' shady ass. Besides, it wasn't like I had not been feeding the dope out to her on the regular anyway, but as usual the greedy trigger went off in her brain, and instead of slowing the fuck down she went over board.

Knowing that I had no other choice, I started locking the bedroom door. I also knew that my mother was always on some ole' slick shit, so I went even further to make certain that she wouldn't be able to get into our inventory, even if she did get in the room. Proving that indeed, she had the skill to walk through wood, my mother went into the dramatics of a conniption fit, when she figured out that I had sealed all entry ways shut on her ass. At that point, I was so through, that I just let her fall out.

In the mean time, with Mac Truck and me both being away from the house so often, the situation between my mother and Mac Truck's Uncle was out of control. Come to find out, Mac Truck's Uncle had been upset about the fact that my mother was around, and felt that since no one other than the two of them were home most of the time, he could call a few of his other family members over to try and intimidate her to leave. One day, the situation got so bad that my mother, was being held hostage in the house by a few of Mac Truck's, drunken relatives. At first, I didn't believe her and I told her that I didn't have time to be playing games, but after I heard the serious tone of her shaky voice, I uprooted from my hustle and headed to see what was going on

Once I arrived at the house I didn't go in right away, but I peeped through the picture window to scope out the scene. Sure enough, Mac Truck's Uncle had his people hyped up on some old western bullshit.

That's when I simply eased my ass off of the porch and went into the shed located in our backyard to get the shotgun. Hoping that I wasn't going to have to kill a nigga, but didn't mind if I had to, I walked back to the front porch, used my key to open the door, and cocked the gun back as I took my first step into the house. Of course, that got everyone's attention. While I stood there boldly holding the rifle in a shot at will position, I suggested that any and everybody who didn't live there should get the fuck out, or I was going to get to clearing out assholes.

Scattering like roaches from a bright light, those muthafuckas got the hell out of dodge. After making sure that my mother was okay, and everything was back on point, I had a short and sweet talk with Mac Truck's Uncle. The whole time the gun was still in my hands, to make certain that he understood where I was coming from. Afterwards I headed back to the other side of town to handle my business. Not knowing that the highlight of my night had yet to make its grand appearance, I got back to the trap to get work. Within an hour, the police showed up with one of my aunties to get my cool ass. It turned out that as always my mother was on some other shit, and though I would never call my mother a snitch, I figured out that, she did lead my aunt straight to me. Her busy body ass was still holding a grudge about me not feeding her any more dope. So when she got wind from a lingering source that my grandmother was looking for me, she sang like a bird.

I was stunned because I had knew that my grandmother was looking for me, but I didn't expect my own mother to rat me out. I could hardly believe what was going on, but it didn't make a bit of difference because I was still pumped up off of what to deal with at the house. I stood bold face at the door and told the police and my auntie that I wasn't going any muthafucking where, and by me being six-teen, there was nothing that the police could do, or at least that's how they played it off. The more my auntie stressed for me to leave with her, the more I put up a fight.

Leaving with eyes that looked like they could laser me in half, my auntie walked away with the police as they stated to her, "Ma'am, there's nothing we can do." That's when I grew some balls and my cocky ass slammed the door behind them. Not considering the fact that my auntie had been dealing in the streets well before I came along, I made the mistake of getting right back to business. I didn't leave the spot, I didn't put a look out outside to case the perimeter or anything that would have required a little common sense.

Before I knew it, my auntie was back on some above the law type shit. I swear when my auntie came back poppin that forty-five, I thought she was bout to take out everybody in the place. Especially once she began to yell out, "Neffe, if you don't bring your ass out here, I'm going to come in there and start poppin off heads one by one. At that moment I released the helium from my head and walked my formerly arrogant tail outside. On the way back to my grandmother's house, my auntie laid me out like her tongue was attached to the trigger of an assault rifle. Remembering who I was dealing with, I was scared to say a word.

When I walked into my grandmother's house, I was prepped up for defense mode and ready to block her ass out. I really was not in the mood to be bored to death by one of her lifelong lectures. What I didn't expect to hear, was my grandmother give me an ultimatum.

Throwing me all the way for a loop, my grandmother began to tell me that she had sent my aunt to find me because she wanted to let me know that she was moving away. She went on to inform me that her job had offered her a better position in Sacramento, California. Finally, she got to her main point of how she thought that it would be good for me to come with her so that I could try to get my life on the right track.

While I stood there and listened to her, I couldn't believe it, because for the first time what my grandmother was saying actually made since. Continuing to process the thoughts of moving away, to get away from all of the mess I had adapted to over the years began to sound really good, and with a voice that spoke from a high pitch that was as weary as my mind and spirit, I answered yes. I generally accepted my grandmother's request offer to leave the grounds that were beginning to stomp me through the mud, because for the first time, I was ready to admit that I was tired. I was tired of fighting, I was tired of the dope game, I was tired of watching my mother tear herself down by getting high, and I was tired of being the supplier that contributed to her self-destruction.

CHAPTER 6

STUCK ON STUPID

The Cycle.

The murders won't stop
The drugs won't end
The liquor store will continue to package
Daddy's little girl will continue to be sold cheap
Without their father
Mother's will continue to search for allowance in their youth
The gang bangers will continue to hold down bars
The innocent will be robbed guilty as charged
The hang out spots will change their names
But the vintage walls still treasures lost souls to hang
The opportunity to get ahead will never fail to be excused
The value of our potential will never out style the price of a new pair of
shoes
The family will never go without a drunk- all can relate
And don't forget the beauty queen A.K.A. brokenly convinced that all hates
The loud mouth will never shut up
And time will run out before the lies
The badgering will never cease on the one that tries
The support won't stick
And sincerity always dies
Nothing is meant to last except anger, resentment, and the will to despise
Trust is the least important quality
And greed is the cause of all lust
Priorities are the least responsibility
And children are the last to get a plate
Thank God for the grandmother's
And pray the parents make the gate
The world will continue to revolve around money as well as nothing else is
known
And self-respect has no meaning
Because self is never known
Intellect has no placement because the mind was manipulated to do just that
Sacrifice holds no purpose because right now is where it's at...S.W.

Moving to Sacramento renewed my sense of pride, and once we got there I was ready to reroute my life for a change. My grandmother got right to work, I enrolled myself into a continuation school, and my grandfather picked up right where he left off. Everything started off good, but it didn't take long for me to become familiar with the land, and before long I was running into the same shit that I had called myself running away from. I had evolved into somewhat of a socialite over the years, so I was able to make friends with some of the fellas at the school fairly quickly. Before I could get settled in good I was smoking, drinking, and fucking at will.

My grandmother's hours of work through the week seemed to be just as long as they were before she moved away. My grandfather was still circulating amongst a galaxy far-far away. Which left me on my own, to get away with whatever I wanted without the threat of getting in trouble by either one of them. It just so happened that I should have been concerned about getting caught up by my grandparents, then maybe I would have played out my decisions with a little more caution, because when I did get caught up, my sweet new start took a sour turn. I was so use to my grandmother being at work during the day, and my grandfather mapping his way around new territory, that I would often leave school early with a so-called boyfriend, so that I could get my grown woman on.

His name was De'Monte and he had a tongue that could make a cat meow like no other, and every chance I got I would take him to my grandmother's house so that he could make me purr. One day in particular, I can remember being in the bedroom with De'Monte while he was performing at peak level, when I heard a set of keys inching in the front door. Scared that it was my grandmother coming home from work early, I pushed him off of me and sent him running out the back door while I ran to the bathroom to clean myself up.

When I left out of the bathroom, I realized that it wasn't my grandmother, but my grandfather had come home early and as I attempted to avoid him on my way back into the bed room, he called me into the front room where he had sat down to watch television. As I headed towards him, I noticed that he had popped one his porno tapes in the VCR, and before

95

I could open my mouth to even ask what he might have wanted, he told me to have a seat and instructed me to pour myself a glass of wine.

My grandfather went on to tell me that he wasn't a fool and that the scent of sex was heavy in the air, and warned me about the consequences of unprotected sex and how promiscuity could lead to unwanted attention. He then went on to say, that he wasn't going to scold me for using his house to fulfill my sexual apatite, but he wanted to make sure that if I was going to be having sex, I absolutely knew what I was doing. Pointing out some of his most satisfying positions while tuned into his personal flicks, he went on to tell me about how a woman should please a man. Not sure of what to think about his approach, I continued to gulp down glasses of wine while he talked and stroked himself to sleep.

By the time my grandmother made it in from work, the house was back to its usual setting. My grandfather smoking a joint in front of the television, and I was lying across the bed. All of a sudden I could hear my grandmother in an intense conversation on the phone, and with the tone of her voice raising the roof she slammed the phone down and stormed into the room with me. Next thing I know my grandmother was cussing me flat the fuck out.

It turned out that some woman from my grandmothers' job had called and told her that my grandfather and I were having sex while she was at work. When she confronted me about it, I was just a stunned as she was. Not to mention, that I was still buzzed up off of the nearly bottle of wine that I drunk earlier, so when she started pointing, yelling, and accusing me of fucking her husband, I was looking at her as if she was a damn fool.

Steadily walking towards me, my grandmother called me more bitches and hoe's than any nigga that I have ever ran across on the streets, and without thinking about the fact that she was my Nanna, I was cussing her ass right back out. Before I knew it, I was standing up in her face, as if she was in my house. I can remember looking her straight in her eyes and telling her how wrong she was for coming at me with that bullshit, and that her husband was the hound she needed to be barking at. I also told her, that I didn't doubt that her husband was out fucking plenty of hoe's and bitch's, I just was not one of them.

The two of us went back and forth for about thirty minutes with no one to intervene, and the next thing I know, my grandmother was packing me up and sending me on my merry way. Without hesitation, she put my ass in another group home. Surely, this was nothing like the projection I had in mind when I decided to make a change for the better, but sucking it up and dealing with the situation for what it was, I learned to make the most of it. Unlike the reform school that my father had dropped me off at when I was younger, this was an actual girls group home.

It was set up with two girls to a room, with only four girls there besides the family that ran it which consisted of the husband and wife, and their seventeen-year-old daughter Ana. They were from somewhere over in the Caribbean's and I couldn't really pronounce their last name, so I simply called them Mr. B and Mrs. B. They were very kind, loving, and caring people who taught me a lot. Especially Mrs. B, she taught me how to clean the house properly, she taught me how to speak a little Spanish, she taught me how to cook Caribbean dishes (especially curry). She also taught me how to be a lady, and most of all she taught me how to run stable household.

While I was living in the girls home, I ended up getting pregnant by a lame nigga that I was fucking with from the continuation school. Not really knowing what to do about the situation, I went to Ana, and after we finished discussing the issue, she convinced me to talk to her mom. I was not sure how Mrs. B was going to handle it, but I did go to her and though she did express her disappointment, she stayed calm and did not raise her voice at me. Throughout the conversation she fixed me some hot tea and proceeded to tell me, how important it was for me to get a good education, and that a baby was the last thing I needed on my plate at the time.

When we finished talking, she sent me upstairs to shower and told me to get a good nights rest, because we had an early appointment the next morning. At the time I had no idea what appointment she was talking about, but when she woke me up at the crack of dawn the next morning and had me follow her downstairs to the kitchen and had me lay across the sheet covered table, I started to figure it out. While everyone else in the house, were sleeping peacefully, Mrs. B gave me my very first abortion. We did not tell anyone, we did not talk about it, and as the days went by, it was as if the procedure had never taken place.

I continued to go to school and keep up my chores around the house, and making sure that I stayed in order, Mrs. B had me on a schedule that was so tight, I barely had a moment to breathe fresh air between the girls home and the continuation school. In fact the only outside correspondence that I had outside of everyone in the girls home was a couple of guy friends who rode the bus with me everyday. Most of the time, the three of us would miss the first passing bus on purpose, just to lengthen our hang out time, before we would head to our final destinations.

One day, we noticed a tricked out Cadillac with rims, tinted windows, and the works. Other than admiring its detail, neither of us thought much of it. As the days went on, we realized that the same vehicle had been circling the bus stop for nearly a week. One day the car circled around once, and then stopped in front of us the second time, and when the passenger side window rolled down, the driver, asked me my name. Hesitating to respond right away, I finally shouted out "Neffeteria, and who are you!", and he responded "Snake Eyes".

As soon as he said his name, Derrick and Justin gave me a look as if the grim reaper had showed up. He then asked me to come over to his car so that we could talk, but heeding the facial expressions from my two friends, I politely let him know that I was not interested. Once he pulled off, Derrick and Justin explained to me that though they had never personally met him, they had heard he was bad news to mess with. Instead of turning me off, that triggered something inside of me that made me want to know more about him.

Over the next week, Snake eyes showed up and waited on me at the bus stop every day, in a hot pursuit, until he finally got into my head long enough to convince me to give him a real conversation. I can remember walking to his car, while glancing back to see that Derrick and Justin were looking at me as if I was going into a death trap. Not really paying attention to the facial gestures they were trying to make, I decided to get in and catch a ride.

While we were heading to the location that I guided him to, Snake eyes began to make good use of the opportunity, and randomly ask me questions about all of the things that I liked to do and what I wanted out of life. Thinking that it was not the time for me to play shy, I told him all that he wanted to know. He then began to tell me what he wanted to do for me, and being that I had fell under the spell of his form of charming persuasion, in my mind, I really wanted to let him. What I did not want, was for Mrs. B to know that I had got my hot ass in the car with a man that I had just met. Especially since she had to give me an in house abortion a couple of weeks prior, so I had him drop me off around the block.

Before I got out of the car, Snake Eyes gently grabbed the bottom of my chin, and pulled my face near to him, and with no resistance to challenge his aggression, I gladly allowed myself to be accessible for a kiss. Immediately, when our lips connected, a spark shot through the insides of me, and turned me on in a way that I had not been in a very long time. Once we finally pulled away from each other, he told me that he wanted to hook up with me that night, and with no doubt about it, I wanted the same.

Snake Eyes and I agreed that we would meet up at the same spot, later on that evening around 11:30 p.m., and with butterflies swirling through my stomach, I stepped away from his car as if, I were being carried away on a chariot. I was so excited that I do not even remember walking to the girls home. What I can say is that as soon as I got inside, I ran to the room that I was assigned to, dove onto the bed, and with my face smashed down into the pillow, I screamed for at least 5 minutes. Fortunately, no one was home at the time, so I did not have to explain my sudden eruption of joy.

I was at the house by myself for at least an hour before anyone showed up. Which just so happened to work out good for me, because I was able to get myself prepared for the evening that was planned, without other noses running up behind me. I emptied out my book bag and hid everything that had to do with school, under my bed. Then I grabbed a change of clothing along with a fresh pair of underwear, just in case I needed to switch gears during my outing.

That night it was my turn to help Mrs. B with dinner, and the greatest part about that was the fact that, I would not be assigned to kitchen duty. Meaning that I would be able to take my shower, and play sleep well before the 10:00 p.m. lights out rule that applied on school nights. Once everyone had completed their nightly duties and went to bed for the evening, I snuck out of the bedroom window and ran around the corner to meet up with Snake Eyes.

When I made it to the spot, Snake Eyes was already there waiting on me, and with a huge smile on my face, I hopped in the car. As I sat situated myself in the front seat, I realized that he had brought a couple of friends along for the ride, but it was all good by me due to the fact that I was just happy to be out of the house. While we rode off into the midnight hours, Snake Eyes, poured me a pint of Gin, and went on to introduce me to his friends as his new girl. Right then, I leaned back into the seat as if I was really with my new man, and took a gulp of the bumpy face, straight to the head.

The night was going great as drank, talked shit, and puff-puff passed, while Snake Eyes drove around the city without a destination. I believe that he was just trying to make sure that we stayed in motion, but as we crossed over into the one o'clock hour, I gestured for a motion of my own. I knew that I needed to be headed back for the girls home before the next hour went by, so with the music blasting through the car, I leaned over to Snake Eyes, and suggested that what ever he had planned for us to get into was going to have to happen quick fast and in a hurry.

Following my lead, Snake Eyes pulled over and told one of his friends to drive, so that we could spend some time together in the back seat.

Fully extending himself to take advantage of the opportunity, Snake Eyes began to kiss and fondle me until he worked my pants down to my knees. Openly, I welcomed the advancement that he made, and the next thing I know we were having sex in the back of his green Cadillac, with his boys in the front.

The feeling was incredible, and even though I felt as though I was on top of the world, I knew that I needed to come down from my high. Aware that it would not be wise to ease back through the windows of the girls home without freshening up, I requested for Snake Eyes to make sure that we could make a quick stop. Totally understanding where I was coming from, Snake Eyes tapped the guy who was driving on the shoulder, and told him to pull over at the next gas station. Of course, that's when my book bag came in handy, station and I was able to wipe myself down and change clothes, so that I could be free of the alcohol, weed, and pussy juice stench.

Again, I had gotten myself all caught up thinking that I was in love, and again it was not long before I found myself in a love hate relationship. From that night on, I was sneaking out the window on a regular. It seemed like every other night, I was somewhere out with Snake Eyes drinking, smoking, and fucking. After a while, I wasn't even concerned about my assigned room mate, snitching me out, because she had a heavy drug habit, that gave us a mutual understanding.

The more our relationship developed, the more Snake Eyes let me into his world. He would even pick me up during the school day, and take me over to his house, so that we could spend some quality time together. That's around the time when I began to feel as though I had an ultimate claim over his heart. However, that was also around the time, when he began to diversify his attention span. Over a short period, I was able to realize that our level of devotion, had heightened to two separate degrees of acceptance, and that's when I went into a jealous rage.

Needless to mention, I had struck out on a mission to fuck some shit up, and I did. The more I found out about Snake Eyes fucking around on me, the more fights I got into. I was fighting wherever, whenever, and whoever. I was fighting on the blocks, I was fighting at the Mall, I even had a couple of fights in school, and the more I fought, the more bitches he would seem to deal with. I even stole on his ass a few times, but when he started hitting me back, I learned to hold back, because I was not going to be able to explain to Mrs., how I ended up with bruises across my face.

I continued fighting to win Snake Eyes love and dedication for about three months, until one day I got ran up on by a girl, who I had smacked down in school. It just so happened that I crossed paths with her and one of her butch built cousins, while at the mall one day, and on sight they got hyped up to jump me. Unfortunately, for them, things didn't turn out quite the way they had planned, because not only did I tear into their ass, but the cousin got arrested for fighting a minor.

When I made it back to the girls home that day, I had a nice long talk with Ana about everything that I had been going through over the previous few months. Not holding back a single detail, and with a look of concern she asked me if I was tired of putting up with it yet. At first, I just stared at her as if I was confused, but as the thought processed through my mind, I responded, yes. I continued to replay all that I had been going through while trying to hold on to some one who had been clearly and openly disrespecting me, and all of a sudden, a sick feeling came over me. That's when something inside of me clicked, and from that point I decided that not only was I tired, but I was not going to deal with it any more.

That day I had refused to take any of Snake Eyes calls, but just like at the bus stop, his charm insisted that I gave him a chance. Finally, I began to open myself up to hear what he had to say, and he began to tell me how much he needed me. He started to stress that he really wanted to see me, and that he wished that I would at least give him another opportunity to make things right between us. After a while, I gave in and agreed to see him that night, only to find out that all he needed to do was get me to his house so that he could fuck me up.

Still to this day, I do not know what had gotten in to Snake Eyes, but when he go me into his house, he went crazy. As soon as we walked through door, he started cussing me out and telling me how much he couldn't stand me. He then snatched me by my arm and pulled me through the dark smoke filled house, until we made it down the stairs to the den area. That's when he hauled off, and back handed the shit out of me across the right side of my face. Once I regained my balance from getting slapped, damn near to the floor, I hauled off and slapped the shit out of that nigga right back. I knew I was no match for him, but I damn sure was not about to lay down for him to whip my ass, that is when he grabbed me by the throat and started choking me.

Snake Eyes continued to choke me until he noticed that I was losing my breath then he threw me down to the couch, and began to rip my cloths off. I was on my stomach, and unable to put up a fight, so I cried out for him to please stop and get off me, but he did not stop. He called me a Bitch and told me to shut the fuck up while he continued to lock me face down to the couch with one of his knees, while pulling my pants half way down my legs. Still crying out to the top of my lungs for him to stop, I could only hope that some one in the house would come to get Snake Eyes off me.

Of course, it was as if we were the only two in the house, because no one even came close to checking on all the screaming and hollering that I was doing, while he forced himself inside of me. Broken down to a helpless state, I was not able to figure out why Snake Eyes was basically, raping me. He was just out to have his way with me by any means necessary, and did not even consider the fact that I was on my period. When he finished assaulting me, I just laid there and cried until he snatched me up and told me that it was time for me to go.

I had gotten myself into a situation that I had no creditable explanation for, and I was in a position where I knew that I had to deal with the consequences on my own. To make the whole situation worse, I found out that I was pregnant. I couldn't believe it, and I didn't want to. It wasn't like I had not been taking the birth control pills that Mrs. had put me on, after she gave me the abortion. At the time, I didn't understand how I ended up pregnant, but I guess that since I was on my menstrual cycle, when the incident took place, the pills didn't work.

I was devastated. I was confused, and I did not know what I was going to do. I was carrying the child of someone who had brutally raped me and knowing that made me sick to my stomach. I also knew that I could not go to Mrs. B for the second time about being pregnant while under her care. That's when I decided to talk to my grandmother into letting me back into her house. I begged and begged and begged until she finally said that it would be okay. Of course I had to sit through a lecture, and I had to listen to her tell me about the rules and stipulations of her household. At the time I did not give a damn what she was talking about because my only concern was to make sure that my pregnant ass would not have to be under somebody's bridge.

Settling back in to my grandmothers' house, was exciting for me this go round because I knew that my cousin Dre was also staying there. We pretty much grew up together in my grandmothers' house, so we were more brother and sister, in my eyes. We were around the same age and over the year's, he too ended up in some shit he just needed to break free from, for a while. Having Dre at my grandmothers house with me, gave me a lot of relief, because I knew that I would have some one to talk to about all of the turmoil that my life was going through. I knew that he would be able to relate to me, and I needed that more than anyone could have imagined.

In the mean time, with the help of my grandmother and grandfather I had decided not to have the baby, because Lord knows, that I thought satan himself had dropped that seed in me. When I went to Dre about my situation, he made it known that he would support me, no matter what I decided to do. He then went on to say, that the thought of me murdering a helpless innocent baby, hurt his heart. I didn't figure it out right away, but after I began to think about his sentimental reaction towards our discussion, I eagerly asked him if he had gotten somebody pregnant. As I suspected he said yes, and knowing the way he had always talked about how he had planned to be as a father, I felt nothing, but pure joy for him.

Still my mind was set on the Clinic, and with my grandmother offering to pay for the procedure, I made an appointment with no second thought. The day that I had scheduled to go in for the abortion, my grandmother was on schedule to be at work for the whole day, so my grandfather took me in her place.

Different from the first time I had an abortion, I actually had time to think about what was about to happen, and it began to shake me so. The nervousness must have been showing on my face, or something, because when we pulled up at the clinic, my grandfather asked me if I was sure that I wanted to follow through with it. Saying yes through a crackling voice, my grandfather lit up a joint and smoked it with me before I went into the building to help calm me down, once I finally went inside my grandfather told me that he was going to wait outside while I went in to handle my business.

As I entered into the clinic, I began to feel as though the walls were closing in on me, and as I put my signature on the sign in sheet, I felt as though I was signing my life away. When I went back to the room for the Doctor to prep me, he asked if I wanted to hear the baby's heart beating, and not knowing the effects that it would have on me, I said yes. I cannot tell you the emotions that ran through me, as I heard the faint thump, thump of a real life growing in side of me. What I will tell you is that I jumped up, and ran out of that place without looking back.

When I made it outside to my grandfather, he was leaned back in the driver seat of the car, and with tears in my eyes, I knocked on the driver side window. Once I was able to gain his attention, I told him that I could not go through with killing my child. That is when he told me that he knew that I was going to change my mind, but he wanted the decision to be my own. He also went on to explain to me that having a baby was not going to be easy, and that the responsibility I was going to have to ultimately carry through on my own.

Now that I had decided to keep my baby, I knew that I needed to contact Snake Eyes. I didn't necessarily want to, but I figured that I needed to inform him about the condition he had left me in, after his psychotic episode. It had been a couple of months, so when I initially tried to reach out to him, he tried to tell me that the baby could not possible be his, and called me a lying whore. At that point, I was determined to prove that his trifling ass was absolutely the father.

The first thing that I did was make an appointment with the prenatal doctor, so that I could request a print out, stating my expected due date. I wanted it so that I would be able to trace the estimated time of birth on the calendar, back to the time of conception, so that I could show him that it all rounded up to the when he raped me.

After allowing the details to process through his mind for a little while, Snake Eyes grew to be very excited about the thoughts having his first child. That's when he consciously made up in his mind, that he wanted to be a part of the baby's life. From that moment on, he became an active supporter during the remainder of my pregnancy. He made sure that I was at all of my doctor appointments, on time. He made sure that I had plenty of food to satisfy my cravings, and he made sure that I did not run into any of his other bitches on the street. He even asked if I wanted to move in with him, so that we could make the family thing work out between us.

Of course, it sounded like a great idea, but at the time, I didn't think that it was. I was content at my grandmothers' house, and even though it was mainly due to the fact, that Dre was around, I thought it would be best for me to stay put. Besides, sitting still for a while being pregnant, helped me to see things in a new light. My perception about life was changing rapidly and now even more than before, I felt like I needed to get myself together for my baby. On the other hand, I still thought the nigga was a quarter short of good sense, and half crazy.

In the meantime, Dre's girlfriend had given birth to their son, and watching his face light up from being a father for the first time, was truly remarkable for me. I loved watching him walk through the house with the look of a proud father. It was like, his life had just begun, and even though he was still living at my grandmothers, Dre was on a mission. He wanted to make certain that he would be around to provide for his son, the way his father never did for him. Unfortunately, his son's mother had different intentions, and told him that she did not want him involved with her or the baby's life, a week after she left the hospital.

Heart broken and mentally wrecked Dre begged for her to allow him to be apart of his sons life, and after a few hours of pleading they worked out some arrangements that would allow him to see his child. They came up with the agreement that Dre' would be able to keep the baby on the weekends, and a couple of days during the week while she worked on completing her senior year of high school. He wasn't very pleased about the situation, but went along with the decision, in order to have a chance to spend time with his son.

During that time, Dre made it business to find a job, so that he could help support his new responsibility. Once he did land a full time position, he would often ask me to help baby sit on days that he had to work while the baby was over. Of course I did not mind, and being that I was about to have a baby of my own, I figured that I had might as well get the experience.

The baby was tiny, but to my surprise, he did not cry much at all, at least not as much as I expected from a six week old new born. Now that I think about it, usually, once I fed, burped, and changed him, he would sleep until he was ready for the next round. One day while I was watching the baby, I walked up the street to pick up a package from a friend of mines while the baby was asleep. I knew that the baby would not be sleep for long, so my intentions were to get back into the house as soon as possible, even through I could see the front door from where I stood. I did not feel as though I had any reason to expect a problem to arise, especially since I knew that I would be close to the house. However, I did not expect, for Dre's baby mama to pull up in front of my grandmothers' house, and jump out of a car filled to capacity, with all of her relatives, only to run inside to take the baby.

Running up to the front porch before she could make it out of the house with the baby, I tried to block her from leaving so that I could find out what was going on. With tears rolling down her face she told me that she was taking the baby away, because her Asian family did not approve of her being involved with a black man. Immediately, I began to plead that she would not leave with the baby. I begged her with everything that I had in me, but she would not listen to a word that was coming out of my mouth.

Hysterically, I ran to the phone so that I could call Dre and let him know what had just taken place. He began to break down instantly, and with my conscious beating me to the dirt. I didn't know how I was going to face him when he got back to my grandmothers house. That night, everything just seemed to get worse as Dre's frustration had him clash with my grandfathers' sarcastic criticism, while my grandmother was still at work. I was still feeling horribly responsible for the fact that Dre's first born son, had been basically kidnapped, while under my care, and cried uncontrollably from the guilt.

The next thing that I know, I was hearing my grandfather yelling at Dre and telling him to get out, while at the same time Dre was yelling back saying how he was tired of being there anyway. When I heard that I ran out of the room and begged Dre not to leave. I told him that I needed him there with me and that he was the only reason I had stuck around so long in the first place. Not trying to hear a word that I had to say, Dre left me standing right where I was and ran out of the house in my sorrow, as I watched him run out of the house in a furious rage. That is when I turned around and looked and looked at my grandfather like, I could have stole on his old ass, and walked into the bedroom to cry myself to sleep.

Shortly after I could hear my grandmothers' house phone ringing, and hoping that it was Dre, I jumped up to answer the call. When I said hello, I was so grateful to hear Dre's voice that I could barely speak without stumbling over my words. As we got into the details of what had happened through out the events of the day, I explained to him how I wished that I could have done something to prevent the situation from arising. He then told me that he did not blame me for what happened, and expressed the fact that though everything seemed to be going crazy, he still loved me like a sister.

Dre, also informed me that he was fed up with all the bullshit that my grandfather dished out. He then went on to ask if I thought it would be cool for him to stay at the house Mac Truck had gotten for me, until he was able to get on his feet. I know it wouldn't be an issue, because the house was still considered to be mine. In fact, my mother was still staying there, so without thinking twice, I told him that it would absolutely be okay. I went on to tell him that I would even send him a little cash until he was able to find another job.

Devastated by all that had erupted, I called Snake Eyes to take him up on his happy family offer and moved out of my grandmothers' house, the next day. I just did not want to be in that house without Dre, and being that I was getting closer to having my own baby, I did not want the stressful atmosphere.

When I moved in with Snake Eyes, I had went out to get a part time job, even though I was nearing, full term in my pregnancy, because I did not want that nigga to hold all that he was doing for me over my head. I did not have any problems getting the job, because even though I was just about due, I was able to get away with telling them that I was only in my first trimester.

Trying to do everything in my power to help our situation run smooth, low and behold, shit still, got out of hand. I came home from work early one day, and this muthafucka had another woman sucking his dick while he was sitting on the coach. Needless say that I went the fuck off. I started screaming at that nigga like I was insane, and when I seen the bitch face, and realized that she was the same woman that he previously introduced to me as his cousin, I slapped that hoe with all that I had in me. Before I know it, the two of us were fighting like jungle cats, while Snake Eyes sat his rotten ass on the couch and laughed as he watched. Clearly convinced that he was totally out of his mind, I could hardly believe that I left my grandmothers' house, only to put myself in a worse off situation. I was so angry, and had lost so much respect for that fool, that I refused to remain at the house another minute.

At this point, I also knew that going back to my grandmothers' house, was not an option, but I knew, that I had to figure out something. I didn't even waste time grabbing a change of clothes. I just walked my disappointed self to the bus stop, so that I could clearly think about what my "due any day now" ass, was going to do. Then it hit me, and I hopped on the bus, and made my way to 73rd street. Once again, to make my way to the Red, White, and Pink house, that never failed to open its door to me. I knew that just like any other time I had gotten myself into jam, I could get out of it, by going to Mia's house.

When I got there, Mia's mother was not home, but Mia didn't hesitate to let me in, and from a feeling of relief, I fell into her open arms. Mia's mother made it home later on that evening, and to my surprise, she was not surprise to see me. She just walked over to the chair that I sitting in, and said "Stand on up Sapphire and let me give you a hug".

Within the next four weeks, I had delivered my first child, and the moment I held her in my arms was the first moment that I believe I felt the true meaning of love. Having a baby was definitely a different experience, but being at Mia's house helped me transition into the role of motherhood very smoothly. Especially, being under the experience of Mia, who had birthed her first child, well before I, was even expecting.

While adjusting to life as a single mother, and just trying to keep my head above ground, I did the best that I knew how at the time, but I really did not comprehend the total responsibility at hand. I wasn't moving as fast as I was before I had my baby, but I definitely wasn't ready to slow down, and I didn't . I would often take my baby for a walk through the neighborhood in her stroller, just to be able to get a breath of fresh air. I would also meet up with a few friends on the block, so that we could hang out while watching the dudes on the block play basketball.

Once my baby turned six months old, I was ready to make another move, because even though Mia's family treated me as if I was one of their own, I was ready to be in a different atmosphere. It was nothing personal, but I was beginning to feel like I was crowding their space. The house was already pretty small, and now that they were trying to accommodate not only me and my baby, but all of the belongings that we ended up collecting throughout the months we lived in their house, I felt like I needed to get out before I wore out my welcome.

Besides, I had started dating and getting a little hot again, so I needed to be somewhere that I could freely express my sexual desires. Of course, my move was to the disapproval of Mia's mother, because she had the idea that the baby and I would stay with her until I was able to get on my feet. I knew that she just wanted to protect me, and I appreciated her intentions, but I felt that it would be better for me to go ahead, and move in with my new boyfriend, and his family.

His name was Boogie, and I had been fucking around off and on over the years, I figured what the hell. His sister also just so happened to be another one of my best friends which made my decision to move in with them, that much easier. I had met their mother a few times over the years in passing, and to me she had always seemed to be a nice woman, so although she was not as affectionate as Mia's mom, I did not think that I would have any issues settling in with her.

Things started off fairly smooth when I first moved in with Boogie and his family, but it wasn't long before the situation began to take a turn for the worse. It turned out that one of the reasons why Boogie's mother was so eager to allow me to move in with them, was because of what she expected to get out of me, in order to help make her ends meet. I cannot even tell you that I had a chance to get all the way in the door good before she came at me with how much she expected me to pay out of my welfare money and food stamps in order to stay in her house. She had totally caught me off guard, but I agreed with no problem, because I had too much pride to go back and face Mia's mother at that point. I guess I also did not mind, because on the brighter side of things being in Shug's house allowed me to be up under him.

CHAPTER 7

BROKEN HEART, BROKEN SOUL

TO BE AS SO

I was like a snake dying on my back
Chocking belly up
I was stuck on stupid but enough of that
Now I'm stepping up
Years have passed and come again
And with the turn of time I've learned to win
For myself
Yeah, for myself
I'm not against me anymore
I've discovered more for myself
Life has plenty for me in store
I've rearranged my thinking
Rotated my values and found myself re-thinking
How about that?...S.W.

Shortly after the baby and I moved in at Boogie's house, he began to treat me just down right dirty. I will not admit that he started hitting on me like the other men I had been in relationships with, but I will say that he treated me as if I was a pest. He began to act as though the very sight of me made him sick, and he eventually left my baby and me living at his mother's house, while he moved in with another woman. He would come in and out every once in a while just to fuck me, and whenever I would try to reject him, out of my anger, he took it.

One evening in particular, he came in the house drunk out of his mind during the middle of the night, and fucked me while I was on my period. I didn't want it at the time, but I also didn't want to wake up everyone in the house by trying to fight him off, so I just let it happen. When he finished pleasing himself, he rolled over and fell asleep, and as I went into the bathroom to clean myself off, I cried because I couldn't figure out why I always ended up with nigga's who just didn't give a fuck about me. Well, it turned out that his little stunt got me pregnant, just like the last idiot who decided to have his way with me while I was on my period, but unlike the last time, I was not about to have another baby without a baby father to go along with it. Needless to mention that this time when I went into the abortion clinic, I did not want to hear any heart beat and I didn't leave out until the procedure had been completed.

In the mean time, I was not the only one finding the challenges of life to be getting extremely difficult to bear with, because during this period my cousin Dre was also, feeling as though each day took a major toll. He never seemed to regain a sense of being ever since his sons' mother ran away with his first born child, so I would often call over to the house, so that I could check on him, because I wanted him to know how much I cared for him, if no one else didn't. Whenever I would talk to him, the sound of his broken spirit would always leave me concerned, because after a few minutes of conversation, he would talk to me about how he felt as though he had nothing to live for and was ready to die.

For the most part I figured that Dre was okay, because not only was my mother around, but Mac Truck was popping in and out on a regular,

115

just to keep an eye out for me. What I did not figure was that, my cousin would end up losing his life, while in the house with both of them. It was told, that he was playing with a gun that he thought was unloaded, but with one bullet still lodged in the chamber of the gun, that he held up to his own head, he blew his brains out in front of everyone that was in the house at the time. That moment in my life was extremely devastating to me, especially since the incident just so happened on my 19th Birthday.

Going in and out of moments, where I found myself feeling very depressed and down in the dumps, Boogie's sister, who was also one of my best friends, would often try to keep me encouraged, by telling me that everything would be okay. She also made it apart of her business to let me known that even though she loved her brother dearly it hurt her to see how much he was putting me through. She went on to insist that I deserved to be treated better than what I had been allowing myself to go through, but it would be up to me to stand up for myself and demand it.

Irritated, not only about Dre's supposedly suicide, but also about the position that I had put myself in, I knew that I needed to make some sudden changes in order to stand up on my own, so the first thing that I decided to do was go to work. Not having any one else that I felt comfortable going to at the time, I went to Boogie's mother and asked if she could help me out with my baby while I tried to find a job. At first, she sounded a bit hesitant, but after taking a few minutes to think it through, she said yes. She told me that she understood my need to be independent, and that she would not mind helping me out in whatever way that she could. From there, she went on to inform me how much more money and food stamps she expected me to contribute out of what I was receiving each month.

Desperate to get to work, so I could find a sense of self, I agreed without considering that she may have been trying to take advantage of me. It didn't take me long to find a job, in fact, I believe I started working within two weeks of me filling out the application. I was just grateful to have a job, and even though it did not pay much, I considered that it was a much better pay than what I was already getting. When I showed for my first day on the job, I was excited and ready to work. Unfortunately, one of the supervisors tapped me on the shoulder and informed me that I was in violation of the uniform code. He told me that I needed to either get myself together or go home for the day.

I stood there and looked at that man as if he was a fool, and before I could open up my mouth wide enough to respond, one of the managers stepped in and told the supervisor that he would take care of the situation. I was still looking around with a dumb founded expression, because I had not caught the bus all the way to that job just to go back to Boogie's house without being on the clock for a check. That is when the manager asked me if I had a driver's license and allowed me to use his car so that I could go and get the proper shoes to work in.

When we got off work, the manager re-introduced himself to me as Elton, and he then asked if I needed a ride home. I responded by telling him that I would like a ride home, only if I had a real home to go to. From that point on, we began talking and the more in depth we got into the conversation, the more we realized that we had both survived some challenging backgrounds. That night, not only did Elton give me a ride to Boogie's house, but before we made it to the house, he gave me a ride in the back seat of his car. After that, Elton and I were nearly inseparable, and soon after we started kickin it, my infant baby and I were living with him and his auntie.

A couple of months passed by with Elton and I pushing to make things work out with each other. Everyday I was waiting and watching to see if he was going to flip the script on me, but at that time of the relationship, it did not happen. In fact, he had turned out to be the best man that I had come across in a very long time. Finally, I was involved with someone who appreciated me, and not only did he treat me good, but he took my daughter in as if she was his own.

Elton was everything that I could have asked for during that time of my life, and as the months continued to go by, I continued to fall deeper in love. Being with him made me feel as though I had connected with my match made in Heaven, and the greatest part about it was that he made me feel as though he thought of me just the same. We did not have anything material to hold on to, but we held on to each other as if nothing else mattered.

Finally, I had come to greet another place in my life where I felt content with everything that was going on. That moment in time not only gave me a sense of relief, and a sense of hope as I looked forward to what the future had in store for me, but one day I realized that life had delivered a unexpected bundle that neither Elton nor myself, was ready to receive. I was pregnant once again, and even though I was pregnant by someone who actually cared for me, we both decided that it was not the right time for us to have a baby. Not having a pot to piss in or our own window to through it out of, we felt that realistically we were not in a position to bring another child into the world.

It was rather difficult on me and Elton, as we arrived to the conclusion that it would be best to terminate the baby, but the both of us figured that it was the right thing to do at the time. Even though our love for one another was absolutely stronger than any other man that I had gotten pregnant by in the past, we didn't want to deal with the struggles that came with the responsibilities another child. Especially, knowing that we were in a situation where we could barely provide for ourselves. I can't say that I necessarily felt good about having the abortion, but for the sake of keeping the stress in me and Elton's life to a minimum, I did what had to be done. At least, just let me say that I did what seemed in my mind to be the best thing for me to do at the time.

Shortly after I had that abortion, I found out that I was pregnant again, but this go around Elton and I decided that maybe we were ready to have our first child together. Besides, it wasn't like we never talked about having a big family in our future, we just didn't feel as though we were ready to have any more children, while we were still trying to get on our feet. In order to help us make a sensible decision, this time instead of keeping the situation solely between the two of us, we went to Elton's auntie to hear her opinion.

Elton's auntie was a God fearing woman, and when she spoke to us about our situation, she was very encouraging. She told us that the Heavenly Father would not put on us more than we could bear. She also went on to tell us that if the good Lord intended to bless us with a baby, then surely He had plans to bless us with the means to take care of it. Just hearing what she had to say made me feel comfortable with the thought of having a baby by the man that I had hoped to be spending, the rest of my life with.

We stayed up and talked for ours that evening and by the end of the conversation, as if she had been reading my mind, Elton's auntie suggested that it would be wise for us to get married. In a mild tone, she mentioned to us that in order to receive the full blessings of God in our lives, we would need to make our relationship right in the eyes of God, before the time came for us to deliver our baby. Nodding as if he was in total agreement, Elton looked at me and asked what I had thought, and responding as if he would never ask, I shouted out with excitement, how great I thought it would be. Not quite certain about how everything was going to come together, Elton's auntie got a few more of his family members together and gave us a wedding.

I was eight months pregnant, when we had the ceremony right in the middle of her front room, and even though we exchanged our vows wearing all black, I was glowing with joy from the inside out. The day was full of laughter and excitement, and thinking back on it, I don't even know how everyone fit into the house, but nearly everybody from both sides of our family, showed up to witness the moment that would mark another significant change in my life. It was truly one of the best days of my life, and just about everyone, that I held dear to my heart was there to share it with me, including my sister, my father, as well as a couple of my closest friends. I was especially surprised to see that my cousin Lesby showed up, even though she was looking like more of a groom than the man that I was marrying, with her girlfriend on arm.

Once the wedding was over, Elton and I got on with our newlywed lives, and keeping to the promises that Elton's auntie told us about, our Heavenly Father sure enough made certain that we were prepared to raise a family when our baby arrived. He was fortunate to get a better paying job, and we were able to work ourselves into our own place. Even though we didn't have much space, it was a place we could proudly call our own. At the time, we were just grateful to be able to walk into another level of living.

Life was great! I was married, my daughter had a father and a couple of weeks after we moved into our new place, on February 8, 2001, I gave birth to our first son. When I delivered Christeon I knew that he completed the "American Dream" family that I had desired to be apart of from the time I was a little girl. He was a gift to behold, through the presence of a tiny package with features that were adorably captivating. All I could do was cry from the joy that I was no longer able to contain, as I stared at his precious eyes, tender toes, strong hands and lengthy limbs. I was older, so my outlook on life was much different than it was when I birthed my first child, and this time when I delivered my baby, I was able to feel proud instead of ashamed, because I knew that what had just taken place was a miracle. I can honestly say that I felt like it was a moment in time that I could truly say the Lord's grace had covered me.

All I can say is that things were great during this moment of my life, but nearly two and a half months later, it felt like hell showed up. Beginning with a day that flowed on a routine like any other day, with my husband and I waking up early to pray before he headed out to work, and ending the next morning with disaster.

During the days while my husband was at work, I would stay at home with the babies, and take care of the household needs. The only thing that was different about this particular day was the fact that It was time to take Christeon to the doctor, for his shots. I didn't necessarily want to, but Elton and his auntie talked to me about how important is was for newborns to have the proper immunizations. I can't tell you that what the two of them were telling me, made me feel comfortable about taking him to get the shots, but for the sake of doing the right thing, I did.

Initially I tried to see if Elton could get off work, so that I wouldn't have to be around to watch my baby get a needle stuck in him. Then I tried to call Elton's auntie, to see if she could be available, but she too was unable to get time off work. That meant that I had to build up the courage to watch my baby, be stuck with a needle.

I was so strongly against immunizations, that my first child had yet to get her first shot, so when we arrived, at the doctors' office, I almost walked out, before I even signed in. I couldn't figure out what it was, but the fear that caused me to run out of the abortion Clinic, while I was with my grandfather, had suddenly come over me. Not wanting to cause any problems with Elton, I didn't allow my mind to get to deep, by convincing myself that it would be over soon.

Once the children and I got back home, the day went on with its accustomed routine of me cleaning, washing clothes, and making sure that Elton had a nice hearty meal prepared when he came in from work. Throughout the course of the day, I noticed that Christeon continued to cry more than usual, but for the first couple of hours, I looked over it. I didn't think that it was a big deal, because I was already forewarned that he would be irritated for a few hours from the shots

However, as the day rounded itself to, I'll say 4:30p.m., Christeon, continued to scream as if he was in unbearable pain. I began to get very scared, so I called Elton's auntie to ask her what I should do. She was able to recognize how nervous I was through the phone, and she suggested that the first thing to do was calm down. Of course, that was hard, as I held my screaming baby in my arms, unable to sooth, or comfort him in any way. Especially knowing that he had never cried that way before I took him to get the shots, that I was convinced to be so important in order to protect his immune system. I probably don't have to mention it, but at that moment calming down was not on the agenda, because I needed to know what the fuck was wrong with my son.

That's when Elton's auntie told me to check the area, where Christeon had gotten his shots. Frantically, I did what she told me, and that's when I noticed that my sons leg looked bruised and swollen. Going further into hysteria, I grabbed his leg to get a closer look, and realized that it was damn near as hard as a brick. That's when my panic level elevated a few notches, and not knowing what else to do, Elton's auntie instructed me to go to the Emergency Room.

Once we got off the phone, I was even more upset than when I first called. I believe that I just didn't know what was going on, or how to fix it, so I chose to not listen to her advice. Instead, I called the doctor, and they assured me, that everything would be fine. They, also told me what type of medication to give him to help ease the pain, and instructed that all I had to do was watch over him through the night. Before I got off the phone from speaking with the nurses at the doctors office, they scheduled me an appointment to bring Christeon in on that following Monday.

Feeling a little more at ease, I held Christeon in my arms and walked with him around the house until Elton came in from work. Thankfully, by the time Elton got home, I had rocked Christeon to sleep. Taking the time to discuss the details of the day with Elton, he pretty much let me make the decision, as to if we should take the baby to the emergency room, or wait until that upcoming Monday, to speak with Christeons personal pediatrician.

It was a Friday evening, and things had settled down quite a bit, so I decided that it wouldn't hurt for us to wait. I figured that, since the nurses were able to assist me with gaining control of the situation, everything would be okay, as long as I followed through with what they told me. Making sure that we would be able to monitor Christeon closely, Elton and I had our baby sleeping beside us for the next couple of nights, (we just made sure not to roll over on him, while making love).

Saturday came and went with everything going fairly well, for the most part. I could still tell that Christeon, wasn't feeling like his usual self, but I did manage to keep him from crying so much, and his temperature definitely stayed down. From that point, I guess I just figured that the coast was clear, and the fact that I had planned to get to church early that Sunday morning for prayer, made me even more confident. What I didn't plan on was to wake up that Sunday morning to discover that my son had hemorrhaged to death.

I can't even tell you that thought of me waking up to see, my beautiful baby boy lying in a pool of blood right beside me, had ever crossed my mind. It was unreal, but at the same time, it was very real. I could not understand it, and once I realized that indeed my son had bled to death, through the night, while my husband and I were asleep, I did not want to believe it. "Please God, don't take my baby away from me", I pleaded as I held my sons lifeless body close to my heart, and rocked back and forth. "Oh, God, please don't do this to our family", I cried out even louder, while my husband gathered up enough strength to call 911.

When the ambulance arrived, they could barely pry Christeons body from my arms, until Elton came over to hold me, as I watched the paramedics walk away with my baby. Not long after, the police showed up to file a report on what actually took place. By that time, I was in no condition to speak, so Elton stepped in to answer all of their questions to the best of his ability. Still not able to accept what was happening, I began to ask God why. It wasn't like we were not trying to live right, but surely the fact that we were at least trying to do the best that we could, counted for something. I knew that Christeon was born with a weak heart, but for him to just, all of a sudden pass away, from a death that is still undetermined to this day, is still to this day, beyond my understanding. I just couldn't figure it out, and I needed to know what I did that was so bad that my Heavenly Father had to take my baby away from me.

At that time of my life, "Never would have guessed" headlined every moment, because even though I knew that Christeon was born with a weak heart, I would have never guessed that he was going to pass away while resting right next to me. I also would have never guessed that I would have ended up, under investigation for his death. Nor would I have guessed that the unexpected death of me and Elton's son would turn out to be the beginning of the end for our marriage.

After Christeons' funeral, everything was in shambles. My mind went through such a drawn out process of trying to figure out what went wrong, and how, that mentally, I was an unraveling basket case. I began to feel as though my life had officially taken a dive into the ailments of a breakdown. The very family that I had prayed for was falling apart and as the centerpiece that held us all together, I became rooted in a certified field of destitution. I seriously zoned out, and the war that was going on within me mentally, evolved to be increasingly unbearable. I was in so much pain that I prayed that God would take my life as well.

I just couldn't cope, and every avenue of comfort that I sought, contributed to the web of self-destruction that spun me into a walking talking zombie. This is the time of my life when everything literally began to fall apart. I went from drinking socially to drinking around the clock, because I didn't think that anyone could understand my pain. This also happened to be the time I drove a wedge between my husband, and all because I wasn't able to understand that he was handling the death of our son internally.

I would give Elton such a hard time because he did not seem to be hurting the way that I was, so I made myself believe that he didn't care. Later, I would find out that dealing with Christeons death was just as hard for him as it was for me. He just chose to deal with it in a different manner, because between the two of us, Bre needed at least one of us to remain strong for her. Of course, I wasn't trying to comprehend no shit like that until I realized that he was fed up and ready to leave me. That's when I started to do everything in my power to keep us together, and before it was said and done, I ended up losing myself just to keep him.

The situation had gotten so bad between the two of us, that I was willing to do anything to make our relationship right again. In fact, I actually started doing whatever he asked, even to the point where it morally tore me down. The next thing I knew, I went from trying to help mend our marriage through church, to opening up the doors for the devil to come in. Things were in such a damaged state, at that point, that the only way I knew how to fix our happy home was to allow my husband to fulfill his fantasies, even if it did involve sin to the highest degrees. Though I'd have to admit, that out of everything that I had done, there is only one thing that I can truly say that I regret, and that's having a threesome with my husband and my cousin.

It's the one thing that still to this day I cannot seem to get over, because still to this day the knife is cutting deep. Even as I am finishing this book, the two of them are still fucking around. She has been pregnant by him and some more shit, and it hurts so bad because I would have never guessed, that two of the people I love the most, would be the very two people to tear my world apart. In fact, as many women that I had been fucking just to keep my husband, no one could have ever told me that he was going to leave me for another woman, especially not my first cousin.

CHAPTER 8

CLOSURE FOR A FRESH START

FOR CERTAIN TO STAND

Of all the things that's going on
That's exactly what I have to keep doing

Of all the temptation that's lurking to divide me from my success
That's exactly what I have to keep pursuing

Of all the set backs that's taunting my process
That's exactly what I have to keep going through

Of all the distractions that's intending to distance me from my focus
That's exactly what I have to keep pushing toward

Of all the pain that gets excited to see me down
Of all the confusion that wants to destroy me before I really come around
Of all the perceptions that get a kick out of seeing me on the ground
That's exactly why I'll continue to rise through
Situations electing me strengthened and abound…S.W.

Of course, we all know that I made it through, but how I made it through will spin off all knew details about who I am, why I am, as well as the direction I'm headed in. So keep your minds open, knowing that just like many of you eagerly anticipate a new season, in order to keep up with my life the way it is. Trust and believe that you will definitely want to find out:

What happened to Mac Truck-

How many women I slept with, just to make my husband happy-

What I had to go through in order to have another child-

How I found out that my husband was living with my first cousin-

What stopped me from jumping over the bridge with my children along side me-

Why I did that caused one of my sisters to put me out of her house-

Why I decided to keep my baby boy-

My baby daddy-

The nigga that crashed my brand new 2008 Dodge, into a Georgia Interstate at full speed-

How the man that I'm engaged to today, stepped in to shelter not just me and my children, but the fool that I was fucking at the time, while I was pregnant with someone else's child-

Why I chose abortion, during my most recent pregnancy-

Oh, and my all time personal favorite, of how I was able to survive being a broke celebrity -

To all of my family, friends, fans, and everyone else who has chosen to read this book, before I close off that portion of my life I would like to open up the fact that I am truly grateful for all, that my life has revealed to me through its never ending process of learning. You see, over the years, I have experienced many different situations while facing multiple life altering realities, and out of that, I will be the first to admit that I may not have seemingly always made the correct decisions. However, I am growing to know and trust, that even though I may not have lived the perfect life in the sight of man, I am living the life that God has structured, to fit, His perfect plans for me. I have also grown to have confidence in accepting the evident truths that no matter where the journey may lead, God has been there along the way.

In expressing that, I'd like you to understand, in your hearts, that I have opened up to you a woman who is still awaiting her full arrival. Know that I have shared with you a story not just based off the life of a television personality or a celebrity, but a story scripted, from the true struggles of a human being. I have delivered to you, through a publicized form of healing, a woman who no longer chooses to live in pain. A real woman, who even till this day is dealing with some real serious life issues, and challenges, as well as triumphs.

I have shared with you a story, to let you know that the struggles you endure can help you prosper, so long as you allow our Heavenly Father to guide you from where you stand, by way of His Throne. I will not lie to you and tell you that it is easy, but I will say that in the end, you will appreciate the turn around, so long as you continue to stand on the truths in His word. In other words, I am suggesting that you should be encouraged no matter where life may have you standing, and know that, so long as you continue to stand on his word, all things out for the good of those who love the Lord.

Trust me when I tell you, that this life is not about pursuing man, and the many idols that this world may entice you to follow, because at the end of the day no matter how many shows you watch, the ultimate reality is that life is real. The pains are real. The scars are real. The downfalls are real. The set backs are real. The children that are abused, and molested, throughout the globe are horrifyingly real. The uncountable families that are ripped apart, by wars stretching from across the street to across the nation are tragically real. Fornication is real, infidelity is real, abortion is real, homosexuality is real, and death in any form is real.

However, once you have figured that out, you can rest assured that the solution to cancel out all of those issues, are also real. It is time for us to stand up, not just for ourselves, but for each other as a whole. We must see, the importance of sticking together so that we can get by and overcome, trusting that we will get by with help from our Heavenly Father we can get by. We can get by, and overcome our wounded emotions and heal because even more so than everything that we tend to chase after in life, God is absolutely, very real.

His unconditional love is real. His loving kindness is real. His faithfulness to never leave us nor forsake us is real. His never failing and always prevailing tender mercies and grace are real. His promise to be there when there seems to be nowhere else to turn, is real. The fact that, He has already seen us out of every situation, before we even know we need it, is my testimony and it too, is very real. Everything about Our Heavenly Father is real, and the blessings that He has stored up for each of us to receive, are just as real as the mess, we allow ourselves to hide behind.

So today, I challenge you to remove the horse blinders and see what is really going on around you. I challenge you to see the times for what they are, and rise up for who you are not just called, but chosen to be. I challenge you, to open up so that your own reality can be an inspiration. I challenge you to walk in the purpose that you have been created for, knowing that if God can bless a lying, drinking, cursing, stealing, killing, fornicating, homosexual, dope dealing, bitching, woman like me, His plans to deliver you are also very real.

Sincerely, Neffeteria R. Pugh

STEPPING AHEAD OF SEVEN PITFALLS

Hey everybody, this is your girl Neffe, and as you have read for yourself in the previous pages, I have shared with the world, just a portion of my life long journey. However, before I officially close out this book, I would like to share a portion of my inspiration to those of you who may have experienced similar trauma and hardships. I am aware that there are many and plenty of people living with the painful secrets of a hidden reality. I understand that there are people with smiling faces and crying hearts that are suffering through their pains alone, as if there is no one around who can relate. So at this point, I would like to list seven pitfalls that many of us slip into along this course of life. Following the pitfalls, and in correspondence with the seven storyline chapters, I will also leave you with seven inspirational quotes that I have been able to use along my journey to step out of those pitfalls, and move forward with my life.

In adding that, I am hoping that you accept my invitation to join me as I continue to grow beyond the incidents and circumstances, that tend to crowd the natural beauty of life. In an effort to assist with the healing of those who may walk battered through this society, I have included a few pages for personal encouragement. The purpose is to experience a form of self-healing through written expression, in a way that I didn't even realize was beneficial until I began conquering my past through pen.

Now, I am asking you to trust me, and use this book as a tool to release your way into your breakthrough. So pick up your pen, to break out of the mold of insanity that has been suffocating our lives from one generation to the next, and release your true Happiness.

Chapter 1 – Low Self-Esteem – You attack a low self-esteem with a high regard of self.

Chapter 2 – Rape Victim?
Have you been raped? Don't be ashamed. That negative energy belongs to the perpetrator. Hold your head high, speak out. Be a survivor!

Chapter 3 – Alcoholism
Alcohol creates a drunken spirit, then leaves a sober mind to clean up the mess. Be Smart!

Chapter 4 – Homeless!
Which is better in God's eyes? The homeless or the Heartless. Don't be lifeless! Give of yourself… Put a smile on someone today!

Chapter 5 – Domestic Violence?
In most cases, the abuser was once the abused. Break the curse!

Chapter 6 – Teenage Pregnancy
What seems like the end of the world; is the beginning of life. Think before you have to take on the responsibility.

Chapter 7 – Death
You don't lose in death; you gain in the eternal memory of the time spent together.

Diary

Date _____

Date _____

Date _____

Date _____

Date _____

Date _____

Printed in the United States
137546LV00003B/26/P